The History of Speaking in Tongues

The History of Glossolalia from Early Christianity through the Present

By

K.D. Johnson, B.A., M.A.R

Charlotte, North Carolina

K. Duke-Johnson

Copyright © 2018 Katherine Duke-Johnson

All rights reserved.

ISBN-13: **978-1798965184**

No part of this publication may be reproduced, stored in a retrieval system on transmitted in any way by any means, electronic, mechanical, photocopy, recording or otherwise without the prior permission of the author except as provided by USA copyright law.

Scripture quotations are from the New American Standard Bible ®Copyright ©1960, 1962, 1963, 1968, 1971, 1972, 1973, 1975, 1977, 1995 by the Lockman Foundation. Used by permission.

Published in the United States of America
ISBN: 978-
1. Religion, Biblical Studies, History
2. Religion, Christian Theology, Pneumatology
3. Religion,

CONTENTS

	Introduction	7
1	A Foreshadow in History	21
2	The Apostolic Fathers	43
3	The Third and Fourth Centuries	51
4	The Fifth and Sixth Centuries	65
5	The Seventh and Eighth Centuries	71
6	The Ninth Through the Thirteenth Centuries	75
7	The Fourteenth and Fifteenth Centuries	85
8	The Sixteenth Century	89
9	The Seventeenth and Eighteenth Centuries	95
10	The Nineteenth Century	103
11	Twentieth Century Through the Present	113
	Conclusion	123

K. Duke-Johnson

The History of Speaking in Tongues

K. Duke-Johnson

Introduction

This study focuses on the history of speaking in tongues ("glossolalia") without regard for differences of denomination. Under consideration are Christian theologians, leaders, clergy and prominent protestant figures in light of their viewpoints through the centuries to the present. Our objective is to trace the occurrences of glossolalia in the world primarily within the Christian tradition without regard for denomination or church dogma. For many believers, the baptism of the Holy Ghost and speaking in tongues is a concurrent event. However, for the purposes of discovery and to follow the tradition from the day of Pentecost, we will attempt to follow tongues through the centuries. The purpose is to show if speaking in tongues occurred in Christian history without interruption and if its practice was a necessity for salvation as some churches and theologians have taught and continue to the current era.. The validity of glossolalia in the present day is viewed in retrospect to the practices of early Christianity as well as other proponents through history. The work begins with glossolalia pre-dating the phenomenon on the Day of Pentecost and examines the experience of the early church claim to authenticity. Two themes pervade the work. First are the cessationist and continuationist positions of those within church history. A second theme is the view of twentieth-century Pentecostalism in relationship to the views of St. Paul as purported in 1 Corinthians 12 and 14, the Apostolic Fathers, Church Fathers and Reformers to examine historical consistency and soundness to the practice of glossolalia.

In the past century, Pentecostalism has expanded worldwide. Its vast appeal in Christianity is difficult to overstate. It is not surprising that this resurgence of the spirit has spread so immensely. It has literally touched every corner of the known world—from China to the most remote villages of Africa. In a day when people are searching for meaning and significance that goes beyond careers and narcissism, people are looking to the transcendent. The lifestyle of the devoted Christian encompasses peace yet a vigorous celebration of God that draws others to desire the experience of communion with the Almighty. The days of the drab lifeless church, as usual, are a thing of the past for many Christians. Accompanying this revival of charisma within the church come the gifts of the spirit. There are nine gifts of the spirit mentioned by Paul in 1 Corinthians 12:8-10.

> "…For to one is given by the Spirit the word of wisdom; to another the word of knowledge by the same Spirit; To another faith by the same Spirit; to another the gifts of healing by the same Spirit; To another the working of miracles; to another prophecy; to another discerning of spirits; to another divers kinds of tongues; to another the interpretation of tongues"

Continualists believe that these gifts are for all born-again believers of the church today. But there seems to be a fixation on the aspect of speaking in tongues and the question of its validity over the past century. A notable theologian on the Pentecostal experience is Walter J. Hollenweger who recognizes that tonguesare an "extraordinary phenomenon" which is "not even spoken in a lot of third world Pentecostal churches" and emphasized that North America placed more importance on the experience of the supernatural than other countries.[1] This begs several questions: What is the place of speaking in tongues (glossolalia) within the life of the church today?" And is speaking in tongues a phenomenon that ended with the apostles with a resurgence in the early twentieth century? Is there biblical support that can support the orthodoxy of the practice of tongues through the centuries and to our present day?

The answers to these questions will verify orthodoxy of supernatural experience within the Christian life today. We can address these questions with a line of thought that if the practice of glossolalia can be proven to have continued from its inception through the centuries by orthodox theologians and Christian movements of history as well as extra-biblical proof that it occurred not only on the day of Pentecost but through each era of Christian history, then it can be concluded that glossolalia is not a present-day heretical phenomenon which has drawn millions of people under its influence and perhaps more importantly, that speaking in tongues can be seen as a testimony of God being current involvement today as He was active in the first century church.

---

[1] Walter J. Hollenweger, "Pentecostalism's Global Language, It's not Tongues but a different way of being a Christian," *Christian History and Biography*, 1 April 1998, Issue 58, 42.

Opposing Views: Cessationism and Continuationism

There are two views concerning glossolalia: The continuationist and the cessationist point of view. Continuationism is the belief that the gifts of the Holy Spirit have continued to this present age, specifically the sign gifts such as tongues and prophecy. Those who do not support the Continuationist view are known as Cessationists.

On the cessationist side, there seem to be two main reasons given for cessation of spiritual gifts after the first-century church. The main support comes from Eph 2:19-20 which has been interpreted that since the church has been established there is no longer the need for the prophet, tongues or healing in the present church and secondly because of the propensity for false teachers and prophets building upon the mystical aspect of speaking in tongues to build heretical movements that deviate from Christian orthodoxy. This will be discussed later.

> "So then you are no longer strangers and aliens, but you are fellow citizens with the saints and members of the household of God, built on the foundation of the apostles and prophets,

Christ Jesus himself being the cornerstone," (ESV)

This cessationist argument has been viewed as misinterpreted by the continuationist as both writings purportedly come from the Apostle Paul's own hand; however, the authenticity of the book of Ephesians has come under scrutiny as being a pseudo-Pauline writing. To view the passage of 1 Corinthians 13:8 as support for cessationist view would be in direct contradiction to Paul's writings to the Corinthian church as well as that of Mark 16:17, although Mark 16:8-20 have some problems as well which will also be discussed later.

A major proponent of The cessationist view was a professor by the name of James David Bales who was a professor of religion at Harding University for over 40 years. He wrote numerous books in opposition to speaking in tongues in the 20th century Church. He states

> "…glossolalia is closer to improvisational Jazz then it is to a language. 1 tons speaker made this comparison for me. The speaker uses syllables the way of musician uses notes. Glossolalia sounds have no fixed semantic meeting meaning. Tongue speakers cannot

communicate specific ideas or fax, but they can use tongues as a vehicle to express themselves in the way music expresses emotional experience."[2]

Another contemporary of Bale was William J. Samarin who stated that he had "...interviewed glossolalia and tape recorded and analyzed countless samples of tongues. In every case, glossolalia turns out to be linguistic nonsense. A person filled with the Holy Spirit does not speak a foreign language, although glossolalia is believed...to be the language of angels." [3]

Many cessationists defend their view that Miracles have seized after the dates of the Apostles. And have determined a phenomenon of the 20th century to be moot and conjured experiences of ecstatic and emotional energy as opposed to genuine supernatural experience. After the Holiness experience and the Azusa Street revivals,there were many who sought to delegitimize the second work of grace evidenced by speaking in tongues.

---

[2]Bales, James D., Pentecostalism In The Church, Lambert Book House, Louisiana 1972, p. 10

[3]Samarin, William J. Glossolalia, Psychology Today, August 1972, pg 49

This mere fact confirms that the act of speaking in tongues had died out from the time of the Apostles through the 20th centuries. Although they were great revivals particularly that of the Kentucky Revival (1850), Cornwall England Revival (the 1850s), the Welsh Revival (1903) and others, the experience did not culminate nor include speaking in tongues. This was new and widely disbelieved not only within Episcopal and Methodist circles but also within Holiness circles. Case in point, the Church of God in Christ, was the result of a church split over this very issue within the Church of God.

The continuationist's point of view is that the gifts of the spirit are for the church of the new covenant and that the gifts will cease at the end of this present age when Jesus returns to receive His church unto Himself (1 Corinthians 13:8-12).

> "Love never ends. As for prophecies, they will pass away; as for tongues, they will cease; as for knowledge, it will pass away. For we know in part and we prophesy in part, but *when the perfect one comes, the partial will pass away*....For now, we see in a mirror dimly but then face to face. Now I know

in part; then I shall know fully, even as I
have been fully known." (ESV)

These differences of opinion as to the gifts of the spirit in operation are not issues that affect salvation (although some Pentecostals sects would say that they do), it does divide the church, and many offshoots of Pentecostalism have been the result. This position adds to the disunity of the church. The problem begs the question, "How does the church reconcile this issue?" This is not an easy question to answer since both sides strongly believe their position to reflect an orthodox position. It is unlikely that there will be any reconciliation of the matter in the immediate future. Although there has been those, who have changed their position to reflect support of the continuationist view which includes some influential sects of the Roman Catholic Church and the Eastern Orthodox Church.[4] Even with these glimmers of resolution, it is possibly one of the issues that will only be laid to rest when the

---

[4] Frederic P. Miller, Agnes F. Vandome and John McBrewster, *Continuationism: Christian theology, Christian, Spiritual gift, Glossolalia, Prophecy, Cessationism, Christian denomination, Catholic Church, Orthodox Church, Pope Paul VI, Pentecostalism , Charismatic Movement*, (Pennsylvania: Alpha Publishing, 2009), 253.

church comes to a final reckoning in the future age with Christ.

The Root of the Matter: Etymologist of Glossolalia

In order to have a proper understanding of the activity of glossolalia, we need to define exactly what it is. We do this by gaining a deeper understanding of the word through parsing its structure and delving into its root meaning. The best way to do this is to go back to the original language, which would be Greek and define the term "speaking in tongues." We find that the Greek word for this term is glossolalia. Just what does glossolalia mean to us now and what did it mean in the early church?

The Encyclopedia of Christianity defines glossolalia as follows:

> "Glossolalia, or 'speaking in tongues' (or simply 'tongues'), refers to the religious phenomenon of persons speaking languages not known to them. The term 'glossolalia' derives from glossai*s* lalo, a Greek phrase used in the NT meaning 'speak in, with, or by tongues [i.e., other languages].' The related term 'xenolalia' is used to

describe glossolalia when the language being spoken is an identifiable language never learned by the speaker."[5]

We also mention here that there are two types of speaking in tongues glossolalia which is the speaking in an unknown tongue. This would suggest that glossolalia could be viewed as a type of unintelligible babble. Xenolalia is speaking in a human language that you have never learned but which you are enabled to speak by the power of God (i.e., French, Latin, Portuguese, etc.). Many of those in the Azusa Street revivals believed in xenolalia but were disappointed in their practice when they traveled on missionary ventures to foreign nations of a different language. We will address this occurrence later in the twentieth-century section.

We do need to mention here that the word glossolalia does not appear in the Greek New Testament. The word is derived from a combination of Greek phrases that unifies the thought of "speaking in tongues. The specific word "glossolalia" is found nowhere in the bible. Gentz notes that the word is a nineteenth-century convention taken from the Greek

---

[5] Geoffrey William Bromiley, *The Encyclopedia of Christianity*, Vol. 2 (Michigan: Wm. B. Eerdmans Publishing Co., 2001), 414.

noun *glossa* ("tongue") and the verb *laleo* ("to speak")[6]

For instance Acts 2:4 in Greek is interpreted:

English: 4 And they were all filled with the Holy Spirit and began to speak with other tongues, as the Spirit was giving them utterance.

Greek: 4 και επλησθησαν απαντες πνευματος αγιου και ηρξαντο <u>λαλειν ετεραις γλωσσαις</u> καθως το πνευμα εδιδου αυτοις αποφθεγγεσθαι

$$\lambda\alpha\lambda\epsilon\iota\nu = \text{they speak}$$

$$\epsilon\tau\epsilon\rho\alpha\iota\varsigma = \text{with other}$$

$$\gamma\lambda\omega\sigma\sigma\alpha\iota\varsigma = \text{languages}$$

The Biblical History of "Glossolalia"

When we examine the New Testament for the occurrence of the word, we find that the idea of glossolalia is clearly brought out. There are four instances of the phenomenon mentioned in the New Testament: (1) Acts 2:4; (2) Acts 10:46; (3) Acts 19:6; and, (4) I Corinthians (12-14) In Acts 2:4 the exact translation of the Greek is "and began to <u>speak</u> with other <u>tongues</u>"(" καὶ ἤρξαντο <u>λαλεῖν ἑτέραις γλώσσαις</u>").

---

[6]Gentz, William H. (General Editor) The Dictionary of the Bible and Religion (Abingdon.Nashville, TN) 1986. Pg 395.

There is also the prophetic announcement of the coming of speaking in tongues in Mark 16:17 "…they shall speak with new tongues." Further, Acts 10:46 also references the idea of glossolalia saying, "for they heard them <u>speaking with tongues</u> and magnifying God. ("ἤκουον γὰρ αὐτῶν <u>λαλούντωνγλώσσαις</u> καὶ μεγαλυνόντων τὸν Θεόν")

Of note, Gentz (as do other scholars), makes the reference that speaking in tongues that initiated the New Testament Church on the Day of Pentecost is quite different from what Christians practice today in that the foreign languages spoken on that day was not the ecstatic religious utterances spoken of in the Old Testament nor for that matter, is it what is practiced in today's Charismatic and Pentecostal expressions.

Other than the Day of Pentecost, the remaining three occurrences of speaking with tongues in the New Testament makes no mention of foreign languages that were understood and interpreted by listeners in the natural. I Corinthians does talk about tongues being interpreted but not as a translation from someone understanding a foreign language. The text seems to denote that the tongues spoken was a heavenly language, not an earthly language to be understood by men. The interpreter was seemingly given an unction to understand and provide for the congregation a spiritual interpretation of a spirituallanguage. Acts 19:6 seems to support the idea of speaking in tongues (heavenly languages as going hand-in-hand with prophecy.

ἐλάλουν τε γλώσσαις καὶἐπροφήτευον.

"…they were speaking with tongues and prophesying…"

The Apostle Paul also gives in instruction to the Church at Corinth referencing different kinds of speaking in tongues and the various spiritual gifts in operation within the congregation. I Corinthians 12: 10, "…and to a different one kinds (divers) of tongues.."

πνευμάτων ἑτέρῳ**γένη γλωσσῶν,**

The Greek word "γένη" is translated as divers in the King James Version but also as different kinds. As referring to languages it refers to those who speak different languages as opposed to speaking just one spirit breathed language. It would seem that Paul makes this differentiation because at that time, there were those who did speak in earthlylanguages which they had not learned. The text insinuates that there were those of Paul's time that continued to speak languages that they did not learn which could be interpreted by those who did know the language.

Discussion and Reflection Questions

1. On the day of Pentecost they experienced xenolalia. In the church of Corinth, Paul says they practiced glossolalia. What is the difference between the two? Have you or anyone you know of experienced either forms? If so what was it like?
2. How wide spread do you believe the practice was in the early church? Is this practiced in your congregation? How accepted is its practice within your reformation?
3. Do you believe authentic speaking in tongues existed prior to Pentecost? Why or why not?
4. Did speaking in tongues add to the potency of the acclamation of the gospel? How is the power of the proclamation of the gospel typified today?
5. What connection, if any, exists between speaking in tongues and the anointing for service?

Chapter 1
A History Leading to History

The Foreshadow of Old Testament

One question of interest is, "what occurrences of glossolalia exists within the Old Testament?" and "how, if any, do those occurrences relate to the New Testament experience of glossolalia?" Within the Old Testament God confused the languages at the Tower of Babel because of the sin of the people.[7] This would be the counter experience of glossolalia in that instead of people being able to be understood, God made it so that people would not be able to be understood. Some theologians compare the occurrence of the Tower of Babel with the Day of Pentecost in that the God did not allow people to get close to him (babel) and restored spiritual fellowship on Pentecost. In the Old Testament, these languages can be grouped because the people were able to separate according to those who understood one another. These were not a heavenly language unto God, but they were earthly languages

---

[7] Genesis 11:1-9.

which could be understood. God confused the language to thwart their attempt to stay together when God had commanded them to be "fill the earth."[8] In addition, they were attempting to build a stairway to heaven to have direct access to God when such access had not yet been granted. Many scholars view the contrast of God's confusion of the languages at the Tower of Babel and the occurrence of the Day of Pentecost as a direct symbolism of God bringing his people back together as well as the purpose of God being accomplished that each person would have access to God. There was no longer a barrier, and the reversal of the curse of separation had been initiated with the coming of the Holy Spirit with speaking in tongues.

There are many prophetical books and occurrences within the Old Testament as a foreshadow and foretelling of the coming of Jesus the Messiah. These prophets have unique characteristics which sometimes included ecstatic behavior, and some would argue that it includes unintelligible ecstatic utterances. Many scholars would make the parallel of speaking and tongues and ecstatic utterances. Ecstatic utterances are made mention of in the Old Testament, and it is argued that there is a direct relationship between said

---

[8] Genesis 9:1.

occurrences and the New Testament accounts. One instance includes the passage of 1 Samuel 10:5ff. To some theologians, this would be one of the early examples of ecstatic tongues (e.g., speaking in tongues). On this occasion, the prophet Samuel was "seized by sudden ecstasy" which caused the people around him to quire "Is Saul also among the prophets?" (1 Sam. 10:11).[9] King Saul also joined a group of prophets playing tambourines, flutes, and harps. The prophet Samuel predicted that: "The Spirit of the Lord will come upon you in power, and you will prophesy with them, and you will be changed into a different person."[10] Von Gorgin tends to agree that the ecstatic utterance was birthed from heathen practices but yet overturned to be used by God for His purpose.

> "The singing and music having been taken up, possibly in imitation of heathen prophets, was to induce more excited behavior expressed in chanting, garbled speech and strange bodily movements. Thus, we see how a God-given blessing begins to be manipulated

---

[9] William Sanford, LA Sor, David Allan Hubbard, Frederic William Bush, and Leslie C. Allen William Sanford, *Old Testament Survey: The Message, Form, and Background of the Old Testament*, (Michigan, Wm Eerdmans Publishing, 1996), p.223.

[10] 1 Samuel 10:5-6.

by men. God still employed them, however, for His purposes. In fact, they were Spirit-led and controlled."[11]

Carson further states that "Unlike the great individual prophets, they appeared to have remained in communities and responded to music with ecstatic behavior."[12] In contrast, some scholars argue for more coherent behaviors from prophets.

While both viewpoints are poignant, Sanford's view seems closer to the orthodox prophetical characteristics. Many of the Old Testament prophets include unusual behavior to illustrate God's truths. Given that God is beyond our understanding and is indeed otherworldly (heavenly) it would seem entirely feasible that He would incorporate that which is beyond humans to minister to humans. Von Groningen is also of the position that there was something supernatural in the ecstatic utterances of the Old Testament prophet which parallels the latter rain of the early 20th and 21st

---

[11] Gerard Von Groningen, *The Gift of Tongues in the Old Testament*, retrieved from
http://www.rtc.edu.au/RTC/media/Documents/Vox%20articles/The-Gift-of-Tongues-in-the-Old-Testament-GvG-4-1965.pdf?ext=.pdf

[12] D.A. Carson, R.T. France, J.A. Motyer, G.J. Wenham, *New Bible Commentary 21st Century Edition*, (Intervarsity Press, Illinois, 1994). 306

centuries.

> Speaking in unison, singing, music by instruments and bodily movements were undoubtedly present as well as some tongue speaking. Evidence indicates, however, that this tongue speaking may have been intelligible as on Pentecost day.[13]

For the continuationist there is an issue concerning ecstatic utterance in that the outpouring of the holy ghost on the Day of Pentecost incorporated speaking in foreign languages which had not been learned as a sign to unbelievers, "for each one heard them speaking in his own language."[14] This was not an unknown heavenly tongue which is widely associated with the Pentecostal faith of today. Many Azusa street missionaries believed that the tongues they were speaking would be understood by people of other languages. This proved to be untrue when missionaries such as A.G. Garr went in an attempt to evangelize India and other foreign speaking countries in their native tongues.

---

[13] Von Groningen, ibid, 19
[14] Acts 2:4 (NIV)

> "Although he had been praising God in an Indian dialect at Azusa Street, when he arrived in Calcutta, India, he found that he had received no special ability to communicate or understand their native language. Many of the other early Pentecostal missionaries would become disillusioned when they discovered that they had not beenmiraculously endowed with a "missionary language," and returned home in defeat."[15]

These failures fueled the early revivalists to amend their interpretation of the function of the Holy Spirit in the life of the believer adjusting their doctrine of tongues from an evangelical tool to that of spiritual empowerment. Although there is well-documented failure of the evangelistic interpretation of tongues for missionaries of Azusa, there are also documented cases for the support of speaking in other tongues within the same time period.[16]

---

[15] Steve Thompson, *A Twentieth Century Apostle: A.G. Garr* from Morning Star Publications; 2004

[16] Ralph W. Harris, Spoken by the Spirit: Documented Accounts of "Other Tongues" From Arabic to Zulu, (Missouri: Radiant Books, 1973). This book gives eye witness accounts of other tongues spoken in the 20th Century.

The Day of Pentecost: The First Experience?

The experience of glossolalia is referenced most prominently in two books of the New Testament, Acts and I Corinthians. In the former, glossolalia was given as a sign to believers as a sign to unbelievers that Jesus had come as the new covenant for a renewed relationship with his people. In the latter, Paul wrote to the church of Corinth to correct errors in the practice of glossolalia in the church. He wrote in response to the congregation in response to their concerns on the matter. A copy of that letter has not survived for us to know exactly what their concerns were; however, we do know some of what was going on in the city of Corinth at the time of the early church which does have some bearing on the meaning of glossolalia. First, Corinth was a prosperous city filled with mysticism and worship of pagan gods. In fact, glossolalia was already in practice in many of the false religions of the day.

Some theologians believe that the practice of glossolalia in the Corinthian church had crept into the church as an outside influence of the pagan practices. What is also interesting is that in no other of the extant letters of the Apostle Paul is glossolalia addressed which leads some scholars to think that its practice was unique to the church of Corinth. This theory is much debated in contemporary theology. The evidence of the multifaceted religions practices lays within archeological finds consisting of many pagan temples worship documented by Pausanias who was a late first-century historian.

> "...wooden images of Dionysus...the Pythian priestess...temple of Fortune...a bronze of Poseidon, a bronze Apollo, a status of Hermes, Images of Zeus...Temple of Hera Acraea, Temple of Aethena, Temple of Tyche, Temple of Apollo, Temple of Aphrodite, Statute of Aethena..."[17]

Second, contrary to popular belief, the phenomenon of glossolalia was practiced by pagan religions and predated the early church experience of the outpouring of the spirit in Acts 2. These practices are further confirmed to not have originated within the early Christian church of the first century and also that ecstatic occurrence predates its formation by over a millennium.

---

[17] Jerome Murphy-O'Connor, O.P., *Good News Studies 6, St. Paul's Corinth Texts and Archaeology* (Delaware, Michael Glazier, Inc. 1983), p.23-26

"...most of these accounts predate Pentecost and were of non-Christian origin...however, the recorded cases of glossolalia go back as far as 1100 B.C..."[18]

This is troublesome for the Pentecostals because the roots of glossolalia lie within early pagan religions. Since the Holy Ghost is given as a sign to unbelievers, the difference and authentic of the Day of Pentecost would be that of the ability of the hearers to understand what was being said in their own language. The early pagan practices do not claim that aspect of glossolalia, and it is thus a crucial point of the early Christian experience which is explained in length by the Apostle Paul and can be viewed as that of Providence for the skeptic.

Ecclesiastes 1:10 states that there is nothing new under the sun and with speaking in tongues this seems to ring true. However, the believers in the new way of Pentecostalism will surely attribute these pagan practices to that of fraud or familiar spirits. The enemy has always mimicked true worship for false worship and sought to copy authentic manifestations of spiritual gifts

---

[18]*Speaking in Tongues*, available from www.speaking-in-tongues.net

with his own brand of heterodoxy. The siege of true manifestations of the spirit has been present since before the beginning of time. We read in Ezekiel 28 how the enemy tried to take the glory that belonged to God for himself. Would we now not think that the enemy would continue with the same devises adapted for the church of the new covenant to veer people from knowing the one true God?

The Synoptic Gospels

In the New Testament, three gospels speak of the promise of the baptism in the Holy Spirit. The first instances are from the Q (Quelle) source. In both the Matthew 3:11 and Luke 3:15-18 passages, John the Baptist who speaks of one who will come and baptize with the Holy Spirit and fire. Scholars agree that Q is a very early source from which the Gospels of Matthew and Luke drew upon to formulate their books. These occurrences merely allude to speaking in tongues and depends upon one's interpretation of being baptized with the Holy Spirit. On the other hand, Mark 16:17 pointedly uses the term γλωσσαις λαλησουσιν. There is, however, some discrepancy with this instance. Scholars agree that this gospel was the earliest of the four gospels and more than likely was used as a source for the gospel of Matthew and Luke. What is interesting is that they omit this promise. The reason for this omission may be that it is generally believed that Mark 16:9-20 is a later addition and would thus explain why it was not used in the other gospels. One of the earliest codices, Codex Sinaiticus (n° ℵ / 4th Century), Codex Vaticanus (B or 03 / 4th Century) and the Syriac Sinaiticus omit the longer ending of Mark 16:9-20. Further, the History of the Church authored by Eusebius and using early church writings also omits the ending. One of the earliestfindings of this longer ending is found in Codex Washingtonianus (W or 032) which also possesses an early date of approximately the 4th and 5th century.

Whether or not the long ending of Mark 16 was original to the text, what we do find is that those who may have added it were concerned about speaking in tongues and the orthodoxy of its practices. They were concerned with miracles and God in operation in the lives of the early church which helps the church of today to examine these practices as authentic and perpetuating within our lives today.

Speaking in tongues is mentioned a total of five times in the New Testament: Mark 16:17 as Jesus' instructions to the disciples after this ascension; Acts 2 on the Day of Pentecost; Acts 10:46 at the house of

Cornelius of Caesarea; Acts 19:6 when Paul was in Ephesus; and, I Co. 12, 13, 14 in Paul's Letter to the Church of Corinth which provided structure for church worship. In addition to these passages, glossolalia is also referred to in Romans 8:26 and Jude 20.

In the New Testament Survey, we learned the political and social climate into which Jesus and the first Christians would have been acquainted. One person of antiquity who was exposed to ecstatic utterance prior to its first occurrence at Pentecost was the Greek Philosopher Plato (428-347BC). In his work Plaedrus, Plato associates madness in holy prayers with "inspired utterances by one possessed and out of his mind."[19] As other philosophers of his day, Plato associated glossolalia with divine inspiration and transcending reality to otherworldliness. A forerunner of Plato was Aeschylus (525-455BC) who refers to the occurrence within his Greek tragedy, Prometheus Bound writing:

> "....once again convulsive pain and frenzy, striking my brain, inflame me. I am stung by the gadfly's barb, unforged by fire. My heart knocks at my ribs in terror; my eyeballs roll wildly round and

---

[19] Plato, *Phaedrus*, available from http://classics.mit.edu/Plato/phaedrus.html accessed on 16 April, 2010.

round. I am carried out of my course by a fierce blast of madness; I've lost all mastery over my tongue, and a stream of turbid words beats recklessly against the billows of dark destruction."[20]

What can Christians make of the pre-Pentecost experiences of glossolalia? We look to Socrates and his student Plato that through philosophy they were in search of the transcendent. They knew that life was more than the here and now and with divine inspiration and the practice of glossolalia they saw that humans could move beyond the here and now into experience of the true self which exists beyond the experience of the now. Through these early examples, we can surmise that ecstatic utterance has always been associated with experience of the transcendent and many historians and theologians have found support of its pagan influences from its earliest record. This begs the question of what makes the Christian experience of glossolalia unique and a true expression of union with God.

The Mystical Aspect of Glossolalia

When examining these occurrences, we see that there is a mystical aspect that cannot be ignored.

---

[20] Aeschylus, *Prometheus Bound*, Claridon Press, Oxford Press, London 1907 p.29

Mysticismin generalhas negative implications. However, Harkness sees it differently and views Christian mysticism as "a direct, immediate awareness of the presence of God, whether in union or communion."[21] A theme that runs throughout the Old Testament as it pertains to mysticism is the idea of "moral purity and the need penitence" as well as the activity of the revelation wherein God imparts his wisdom to an individual in a miraculous way.[22] Referring to the Old Testament Harkness says that:

> "The mystic looks to God in praise and prayer and hopes for a vision of God that will enable him to live more fruitfully and faithfully."[23]

This perspective is akin to the occurrence of Acts 2 where the 120 were gathered in the upper room in Jerusalem in prayer and where awaiting the promise "vision of God" that was to empower them for service (fruitfulness in service) and to give them power (Greek *dunamis*) to live faithfully and courageously for Christ (Acts 1:4ff).

---

[21] Gloria Harkness, *Mysticism, Its Meaning and Message* (Tennessee: Abingdon, 1973), 35.
[22] Ibid., 36-8.
[23] Ibid., 38.

What we find in both the old and New Testament is man's desire for the transcendence of God—the desire for God's spirit active and engaged in the lives of mortal humans. Although the Holy Spirit was not yet given as the prophet Joel had prophesied, we see the Holy Spirit active as a prelude to what was to come and foretold in Joel 2:28.

> "…And afterward, I will pour out my Spirit on all people. Your sons and daughters will prophesy, your old men will dream dreams, your young men will see visions." (NIV)

Further, we see in Isaiah 28:11 "Indeed, He will speak to this people through stammering lips and a foreign tongue."This is the foretelling of glossolalia which was also quoted by the Apostle Paul in I Cor. 14:20-22. In this portion of his epistle, he is teaching the church of Corinth on the activity of glossolalia within the congregation and quotes the prophet Isaiah to validate the occurrence of this practice. This is indicative of the fact that when the day of Pentecost came, the people who heard them were confused and did not understand what was going. This is reminiscent of Isaiah decreeing the judgment of God upon the Assyrians and as a sign that God was with the Israelites in parallel to the new covenant with the Israelites being judged for their rejection of Jesus and now being with the Christians.

Although the people of Corinth were engaged in many heretical religions and practices, which also practiced glossolalia, they valued speaking in tongues as a gift of God which they desired. The church of Corinth, however, desired these miraculous gifts disproportionately higher than other gifts and Paul is forced to send a corrective letter to get the church back on track. Fundamentalist Cessationists such as John R. Rice seem to take it a bit further and refer to tongues as heresy within the church. He goes on to discredit the practice of glossolalia and interprets 1Cor 14:23ff as Paul's denouncement of speaking in tongues.

> "…how ridiculous it would appear to unsaved and unlearned strangers to be in a service in which people talked languages that could not be understood. That would be obviously foolish and wrong."[24]

Still, others opine that the activity of glossolalia

---

[24] John R. Rice, *Commentary on I and II Corinthians, The Church of God at Corinth*, (Tennessee, Sword of the Lord Publishers, 1973), 136.

was due to the influence of pagan religions who practiced speaking in tongues and that this activity was infiltrated within the church. These views, however, do not take into consideration that the letter to the Corinthian church, being one of the undisputed letters of Paul, wherein he states that he too spoke in tongues more than they. Speaking in tongues was not unique to the church of Corinth. In fact, the first occurrence of speaking in tongues within orthodoxy was with the 120 in the upper room in Jerusalem as told in Acts 2.

First Century Church and Glossolalia

The first support Pentecostals would find is that glossolalia was prophesied in Joel 2:28 and fulfilled in Acts 2. The gift of the spirit was given according to the will of God. After Jesus' ascension to heaven, he knew that believers would need power and authority to continue His work on the earth. He sent the Paraclete to walk alongside people to help and strengthen his people to live this life. Jesus was the fulfillment of the law and with that fulfillment; he was indeed this new covenant. With this new covenant, which was foretold in the Old Testament he sealed his people as his own. Paul admonishes:

> "… do you not know that your body is a temple of the Holy Spirit within you, whom you have from God? You are not your own, [20] for you were bought with a price. So glorify God in your body." (1Co. 6:19-20, ESV)

Dr. Van Elderen supports the indwelling and purpose for being filled with the spirit as being that of a witness to others and for self-edification in prayer. Thus, the speaking in other tongues has value to others as opposed to speaking in unknown tongues as helpful for the believer's intimacy with God in prayer.

> "Hence, in view of the parallel situations, one can conclude that the speaking with tongues served the same purpose in both cases - validation, confirmation, authentication [and] edification…."[25]

This point is further explained by Paul as it seems that the original purpose of tongues had taken on

---

[25] Bastian Van Elderen, "Glossolalia in the New Testament" *Bulletin of the Evangelical Theological Society 7*, no. 2 (1964) p.55-6 available from http://www.biblicalstudies.org.uk/pdf/bets/vol07/7-2_elderen.pdf, accessed on 2 March, 2010.

a different connotation early on in the Christian church. A shift in the purpose of tongues seems to have taken place in relation to the occurrence on the Day of Pentecost. This fact may also be paralleled by the new wave of Pentecostalism experienced by the holiness movement of the late 19th and early 20th century. Could it be that the early church also experienced failure in their efforts to use xenolalia in their early evangelistic efforts just as those of the early Pentecostal movement? We can find no supporting documentation for this hypothesis, but there are some similarities as we move from ecstatic utterances of foreign languages to that of heavenly languages.

A question comes to the forefront when pondering this possibility since we are to follow the model of the apostles, would it be proper to expect the same enabling gifts to serve the Lord in the fullness of His calling? This question can be addressed in light of Act 2 as a fulfillment of Joel 2:28 "It shall come to pass in the last days, saith God, I will pour out of my Spirit upon all flesh, and they shall prophesy." This verse seems to imply that the Spirit is for all flesh. Not just for those who were alive at the time of the inception of being filled with the Spirit. When viewing all scripture relevant to glossolalia, it appears that the gift was given both as a sign to unbelievers (which we see very little of today) and for edification in prayer as spoken of by Paul. Paul states in 1 Co. 14:18 "He that speaketh in a tongue, speaketh not unto men, but unto God . . . but he that prophesieth, speaketh unto men unto edification." I thank my God I speak with all your tongues."

Discussion and Reflection Questions

1. Did speaking in tongues occur in the Old Testament?

2. Why should Christians study the history of glossolalia?

3. What would be your apologetic defense relating to the continualist/cessationist view of speaking in tongues?

4. How does speaking in tongues relate to the conversion experience?

5. What was the original purpose of the gift of tongues in the early Church?

6. Depending upon your position, what response would you give to those who do not speak in tongues or conversely those who do speak in tongues?

7. In your opinion, is it biblical for believers to speak in tongues today? why / why not?

Chapter 2
The Apostolic Fathers

In Bible Interpretation we learned the importance of getting to the root of the matter when doing exegetical study. Accordingly, we turn to the words and writings of the apostolic fathers to root out their view on glossolalia within early church practices. During our study of Church History (Both I and II) there was little to no mention of glossolalia until we came to the Azusa Street Revivals of 1906, which will be discussed later. One widely accepted reason for the sparse mention of glossolalia in the early church is because the church was under a lot of scrutinies and suffered persecution since they did not follow the customs and practices of the Greco Roman world.

They did not practice idol worship which many viewed then as peculiar. The rituality of glossolalia would have added to thembeing condemned in the public eye. The church fathers, such as Ignatius were attempting to build the church and their acceptance within society and speaking in tongues would not have aided in that attempt.[26] Upon further investigation, however, there is some reference to its acceptance in the Apostolic Fathers in a very early church writing. The Didache does make mention of *speaking in the spirit*, although there is disagreement among scholars as to its interpretation since the original Greek uses lalounta en pneumati (inspired speaking) and does not use the term glossolalia which would refer to speech in language.

> "….but if he ask money, he is a false prophet. And any prophet speaking in the Spirit ye shall not try neither discern; for every sin shall be forgiven but this sin shall not be forgiven. Yet not everyone that speaketh in the Spirit is a prophet, but only if he has the ways of the Lord." [27]

In fact, Aaron Milavec denies that we are dealing with glossolalia and goes on to say that "nor should it should be supposed that 'speaking in the Spirit'

---

[26] Morton T. Kelsey, Tongue Speaking: An Experiment in Spiritual Experience, (New York: Doubleday & Company, 1964), 33.

[27] Didache, 11:9-11. Available from www http://www.earlychristianwritings.com/text/didache-lightfoot.html accessed 24 March, 2010.

necessarily implied some paranormal ecstatic state wherein voluntary control was surrendered to the 'Holy Spirit.' Though he denies this aspect, he does concur that "speaking in Spirit" is speaking under the influence of the Holy Spirit.[28] The question then remains that given the early dating of the Didache, 50-70AD, that it may still refer to glossolalia since during the early church it was frequently associated with the prophetic. Such was the case in Paul's writing to the church of the Corinth when he was setting the occurrence in order.[29]

The protestation of glossolalia was first experienced from outsiders of the church and later insiders. Both Ignatius and Irenaeus, however, spoke in support of the practice within the church, although the practice was viewed more as personal spiritual edification and associated within prophecy within the church as opposed to public displays outside of the church.[30]

Ignatius' date from 80-140 A.D. (others date it more precisely to 95-96AC) makes reference to glossolalia in his day in his letter to the Corinthians

---

[28] Aaron Milavec, The Didache: Faith, Hope & Life of Earliest Christian Communities 50-70 C.E., (New Jersey: The Newman Press, 2003), 458.
[29] I Corinthians 12-14.
[30] Kelsey, 35.

saying that "the holy spirit was poured out in abundance on you all." [31]   Here it seems that Clement may have been referring to the writings of Paul and reminiscing over the charisma of the church and how they have fallen away from the things of God. This would seem to infer that Clement knew of the Holy Spirit's working within the church of Corinth and wanted them to return to their former ways which would have included speaking in tongues.

Irenaeus of Lyons who dates from circa 115-202 AD states "In like manner do we also hear many brethren in the church who possess prophetic gifts, and who through the Spirit speak all kinds of languages, and bring to light, for the general benefit, the hidden things of men and declare the mysteries of God, who also the apostles term spiritual."[32]

Further, Irenaeus recorded an incident of speaking in tongues which he believed to be heretical. In "Against Heresies" Irenaeus reports of a man named Marcus who he perceives to be somewhat of an Antichrist. He and his followers were charged with emotional excesses and moral abuses.

---

[31] Clement. *First Epistle of Clement to Corinthians*, 1Clem 2:2 Available from http://www.earlychristianwritings.com/text/1clement-lightfoot.html retrieved on 24 March 2010

[32] Irenaeus, *Against Heresies*, Book V, vi.

"He [Marcus] deceived many and (has) drawn them in his train... [Marcus says to the woman] open your mouth and prophecy.' But the woman replies, 'I never prophesied; I don't know how to prophesy.' Then he offers some invocations a second time, to the amazement of the deceived woman, and says to her, 'Open your mouth and say whatever comes, and you will be prophesying,' Made flighty and gulled by what has gone before, her soul overheated in the expectation of being about to prophesy, her heart beating wildly *she dares to speak inanities, to say everything which comes to her, rashly and emptily, flushed with the warmth of that vain spirit;* and henceforth she regards herself as a prophet and gives thanks to Marcus who has shared his Grace with her.[33]

Further support of the continuance of glossolalia within the second-century church was that of Justin Martyr (circa A.D. 150) who stated "For the

---

[33] Ibid, III, xiii

prophetical gifts remain with us, even to this present time.[34] These witnesses and others of the apostolic fathers support the continuance of glossolalia within the church. Although glossolalia is not discredited its practices are guarded as Christian leaders seek to keep Christianity alive and look to be accepted within mainline society.

From the Apostolic Fathers, we see that Glossolalia was alive and well in the church, however, there was growing apprehension in the hierarchy of the church as to its practice because of how the church would be viewed and their acceptance within society. They associated glossolalia with the graces of God and with prophecy. The term glossolalia was frowned upon both inside and outside of the church. It seems that the more secular the church became, the more the gifts of the spirit waned. The more the church attempted to fit into the world's way of doing things the less we see of this spiritual manifestation. It can be viewed from a spiritual aspect that God's presence within those who were trying to fit was departing and this become more widespread within the church body itself. The more the church fell away from Paul's perspective to be a peculiar people and a royal people the less we see of the gifts of

---

[34] Justin Martyr, *Dialogue with Trypho*, Chap LXXXII.

the spirit in operation in the church.

Discussion Questions

1. Which of the apostolic fathers were cessationists? Which apostolic fathers were continualists?

2. How radical did Christians have to be in light of Roman beliefs? Could they express their faith without reprisal?

3. How would you have lived out your faith if you lived during the second and third centuries?

K. Duke-Johnson

Chapter 3
The Third and Fourth Centuries

One of the reasons that the church did not embrace tongues in the early church was because there was a tendency for many to misappropriate the gift. This led to divisions and unorthodox teachings. Tertullian of Carthage of the Third Century A.D. was a Christian apologist and is noted as being the father of Latin Christianity.[35] In 207 Tertullian wrote concerning the gifts of the spirit in operation in his day to refute Marcionism. In particular, he wrote concerning the gift of the interpretation of tongues in refuting the heretical teaching of Marcion.

> "...Let Marcion then exhibit, as gifts of his god, some prophets, such as have not spoken by human sense, but with the Spirit of God, such as have both predicted things to come, and have made manifest the secrets of the heart; let him produce a psalm, a vision, a

---

[35] Ekonomou, Andrew J., *Byzantine Rome and the Greek Popes: Eastern influences on Rome and the papacy from Gregory the Great to Zacharias, A.D. 590-752*. (Maryland, Lexington Books, 2007), p 22.

prayer -- only let it be by the Spirit, in an ecstasy, that is, in a rapture, whenever an interpretation of tongues has occurred to him; let him show to me also, that any woman of boastful tongue in his community has ever prophesied from amongst those specially holy sisters of his. Now all these signs (of spiritual gifts) are forthcoming from my side without any difficulty...")[36]

Origen (185–254 A.D.), a theologian of the early church of the third century, was a continuationist who stated in his Commentary on I Corinthians 4:52 "Tongues will cease when I express what I want to say with my mind." He further comments in agreement with the Apostle Paul on the orderliness in speaking in tongues in the church of his day and refers to the lesson to the Corinthian church spoken of in First Corinthians 14. "If the one who speaks in tongues does not have the power to interpret them, others will not understand, but he will know what he was moved by the Spirit to

---

[36] Tertullian, *Tertullianus Against Marcion: Ante Nicene Christian Library Translations of the Writings of the Fathers Down to AD 325* Part Seven, Book V, Chapter VIII, ed. Alexander Roberts (Montana: Kessinger Publishing , 2004) , 411.

say."[37] Although there are some references to glossolalia during this time, there was also the growth of heretical movements of mysticism claiming to be Christian and giving a bad name to the church. With demonstrations of the gift within orthodoxy, we cannot ignore the heretical practices of ecstatic utterances of the day which may have lent itself to many of the church leaders' movement to cease its practice along with the false teachings of the day. They may have felt that it was safer not to place such focus on its practice due to this fact and to protect the neophytes of the church from becoming caught up in false doctrine.

To add to the debate are the writings of St. John Chrysostom (347-407A.D.) who was the Bishop of Constantinople. He was a contemporary of Eusebius and St. Athanasius and would have been familiar with the effects of the Nicene Council. During this time, it seems as if there was an ongoing debate about glossolalia being that he addresses it in his writings by asking a question that he knows the answer to. "If speaking in tongues is useless, why was it given? It was given for the benefit of the person who has it."[38]

---

[37] Origen, *Commentary on I Corinthians* 4.61-62.
[38] John Chrysostom, *Homilies on the Epistle of Paul to the Corinthians 35.4*, Available from

By this example, Chrysostom two points concerning his position on glossolalia are revealed. First, that he believed that speaking in tongues was for self-edification and therefore spoken unto God. This may infer that he held to a heavenly language as well as that of foreign languages because he goes on within the same homily to state:

> "Whoever was baptized in apostolic days, he straightway spoke with tongues, for since on their coming over from idols, without any clear knowledge or training in the Scriptures, they at once received the Spirit and one straightway spoke in the Persian language, another in the Roman, another in the Indian, another in some other tongues, and this made manifest to them that were without that it was the Spirit in the very person speaking. Wherefore the apostle calls it the manifestation of the Spirit which is given to every man to profit withal." [39]

---

http://www.ccel.org/ccel/schaff/npnf109.iii.i.html?highlight=ohn,chrysostom,homilies,on,the,epistle,of,paul,to,corinthians#highlight

[39] Chrysostom, 35.1

Chrysostom agreed with the view that speaking in tongues was not only for the apostles but was a present-day manifestation. However, his belief was that the church had fallen away from possessing the gift. This testimony dates to his time of the late fourth and early fifth centuries which lets us know that this decline was early in nature. "...

Another slightly ambiguous testimony of the continuatist view is that of St. Cyprian (AD248-258) who testifies of the evidence of others which whom he prayed as "...those baptized into the Church being brought to the bishops of the Church, and by our prayer and laying on of hands they receive the Holy Ghost, and are perfected with the seal of the Lord." (Ep.Lxii.8; Ep. Lxxv.7,8)[40]

The seal of the Lord of which Syprian is speaking is believed to be the evidence of speaking in tongues for who else could Cyprian bear witness that they had received the Holy Ghost.

There are other less prominent writers on glossolalia during this period which is available; however, the final witness we shall explore of the fourth century is that of St. Augustine of Hippo. Much has

---

[40] Cutts, Edward Lewes, A Dictionary of the Church of England, Pg. 195

been said of Augustine pertaining to his beliefs and the influence upon modern Christianity, however, like other scholars of his day, his emphasis on doctrine lies not with speaking in tongues but on the grace of God through the Holy Spirit. What he does say about glossolalia is minimal and lies with the continualist point of view as well as the position that on the Day of Pentecost, those who were gathered spoke in intelligible languages which could be understood. Thomas Aquinas agrees with Augustine as he quotes him in Summa Theologica referring to Augustine's Tract XXXII in Joan:

> "Whereas even **now** the Holy Ghost is received, yet no one speaks in the tongues of all nations because the Church herself already speaks the languages of all nations: since whoever is not in the Church, receives not the Holy Ghost."[41][42]

Although Augustine does not believe in the discontinuance of other tongues, there is a statement

---

[41] Thomas Aquinas, *Summa Theologica*, Art. 1., Available from , http://www.ccel.org/ccel/aquinas/summa.SS.iv.SS_Q176.SS_Q176_A1.html?highlight=augustine,tract,xxxii,in,joan,speaks,the,languages#highlight accessed 20 April, 2010.

[42] Augustine of Hippo, *The Gospel of John, Tractate 32*

that is used by those who desire to state that Augustine was a continuance. Many on the internet use the following to support this view; however, the researcher can find no supporting primary sources to validate this point. Thus we must conclude that Augustine was a cessationist as the following quote (which is much referred to on the internet) cannot be authenticated as Augustine.

> "We still do what the apostles did when they laid hands on the Samaritans and called down the Holy Spirit on them in the laying-on of hands. It is expected that converts should speak with new tongues." [43]

There are, however, other citations which could put Augustine's point of view on the matter in question. For instance, Augustine comments on spiritual occurrences stating "…for not everyone has all of them [gifts of the spirit], but some have these and others those, although each has the Gift himself…"[44] From reliable sources, such as Augustine, we can conclude that during this era, glossolalia was indeed in operation

---

[43] "Did Augustine Speak in Tongues?," *Grace Forums*, Available from http://www.graceforums.com/printthread.php?tid=2312 accessed on 19 April 2010

[44] Augustine of Hippo, Trinity 15.

within the church. Although not all church fathers agreed, the existence of its practice within the Christian arena yet remains. Another testimony is that of Severian Bishop of Gabala (Syria) in the late fourth and early fifth century. He was in favor of speaking in tongues in his day. He stated in his Commentary that "...Tongues are a miracle in themselves. Prophecy, however, is a miracle in the substance of what it contains but not in the way in which it is uttered."[45] Kelsey notes that one of the final eyewitness accounts of glossolalia is given by a fifth-century history named Sozomen, he tells of the Egyptian abbot, St. Pachomius (a friend of St Athanasius) who spoke "the language of angels" and had a "sudden spurt of Greek and Latin, tongues he had never had time to study."[46]

As the fourth century comes to a close the church and becomes the official religion under Constantine and continues to take on the embodiment of power and prestige in church government, we see that other issues of dogma take the front center stage. Issues of soteriology and Christology are issues that the

---

[45] Severian of Gabala, *Pauline Commentary From the Greek Church. Ancient Commentary on Scripture, 1 & 2 Corinthians* Eds Gerald Bray and Thomas C. Oden,(Illinois: Dearborn Publishers, 1999), p.51.
[46] Kelsey, 38.

church seeks to answer. These theological questions, although important and of concern to the church, seem to take on more significance than the experience of God on a personal level. In fact, it increasingly became the position of clergy that only the common man was unable to understand the things of God. Also at issue was human's quest for knowledge concerning the nature of God and the hard questions of Christianity. Humanity seeks for Christ to make sense to them, but for this knowledge, the church seems to lose the essence of fellowship with God.

G.R. Osbourne, notes that there was a decline in "supernatural gifts" (speaking in tongues) in the western church during the fourth century and following.[47]

The Heretical Movements

It should be noted that there were many heretical movements that attached themselves to the Pentecostal experience. These movements date from early Christianity. We see this evident in the New Testament in the occurrence of Simon the magician who wanted the spiritual gifts that Peter had. Paul also warns in his letters against false teachers who came in

---

[47] Osbourne, G.R., Evangelical Dictionary of Theology (Elwell, Walter G., Editor) Baker Books, Grand Rapids, MI, Pg 1102

the name of the Lord (1 Tim. 6, 2 Tim. 3:11ff). Many offshoots of Christian were categorized by the early Christians as heretical.

One of the early movements that attached itself to Christianity and the gifts is also associated with one of the Apostolic Fathers. Tertullian took on Montanism towards the end of his life. Early Montanists claimed speaking in tongues and the gift of prophecy which were deemed almost the same as the early Christian movement. They claimed to speak in tongues but were widely known by the church to have evolved into heterodoxy due to their lack of organization and errors in interpretation of scripture. Schaff quoting Asterius Urbanus writes that at times Montanists would become overcome with seizures, fall into trances and spoke in unknown tongues.

> "…and suddenly being seized with a kind of frenzy and ecstasy, he raved, and began to speak and to utter strange things, and to prophesy in a manner contrary to the custom of the Church …For he stirred up two others also, women, and filled them with the spurious spirit, so that they too spoke in a frenzy and unseasonably, and in a

strange manner..."[48]

Gnosticism is also another heretical divergent with claims Christian roots. With the discovery at Nag Hammadi different more radical gospels have surfaced (i.e., the Gospel of the Egyptians) and their mystical practices have been associated with the early Church but are full of heterodoxy. Some associate the introductory prayer of the Gospel of the Egyptians as one early form of written glossolalia outside of early Christianity.

> "...Ié ieus éó ou éó óua! O Jesus, bond of Yah's righteousness, O Living Water, O Child of Child, O glorious Name! Really truly, O Eon that is, iiii éééé eeee oo uuuu óóóó aaaaa, really truly éi aaaa óó óó! O One That Is, Seer Of the Ages! Really truly, aee ééé iiiiuuuuuu óóóóóóóó, You who are eternally eternal, really truly iéa aió, in the heart, You who Are, You are what

---

[48] Philip Schaff, *Fathers of the Third and Fourth Centuries: Lactanius, Venantius, Asterius, Victorinus, Dionysius, Apostolic Teaching and Constitutions, Homily,* Vol. 7, available from http://www.ccel.org/ccel/schaff/anf07.v.ii.html accessed on 22 April 2010.

You are, ei o eieiosei!"[49]

Messalians (360 A.D. – 800 A.D.) is another one of the many heretical movements whose movement lasted over 400 years. They believed that everyone was possessed by demons and the only way to rid themselves of this malady was to be filled with the Holy Spirit. The way that people were to receive this baptism was by the laying on of hands.[50]

It is important to mention these heretical movements to show that many other religions were extant that combated with the survival of the early church. The existence of these unorthodox teachings and practices lends further support as being one of the reasons why the Apostolic Fathers and the Early Christian Fathers veered away from unusual ecstatic activity within the church.

For unbelievers, it seemed difficult to differentiate the true manifestation of the spirit from the heretical. Thus, to secure the survival of Christian

---

[49] The Gospel of the Egyptians – T*he Nag Hammadi Library*. *The Gnostic Society Library,* available from http://www.gnosis.org/naghamm/goseqypt.html accessed on 22 April 2010.
[50] Stanley M. Burgess, Eduard M. van der Maas, Ed van der Maas, *The New International Dictionary of Pentecostal and Charismatic Movements*, (Michigan: Zondervan, 2002),1228.

in a time when Christianity was already viewed as divergent from the societal polytheistic belief, they suppressed glossolalia.

Discussion and Reflection Questions

1. What part did fanaticism play in the practice of glossolalia?

2. What part, if any, did Gnosticism play in the spread/practice of speaking in tongues?

3. Accusations of fanaticism was an problem in the early church. How did glossolalia contribute to that thought? How is the practice viewed today? In what ways can continualists protect their orthodoxy without ceasing to be true to their convictions of being spirit filled in the post modern era?
4. What other practices of the early church were considered fanatical by the Roman world?
5. Can you cite specific instances where church fathers differed in opinion concerning the manifestation of speaking in tongues? Which Bishop was the most vocal in his persuasion?

Chapter 4
The Fifth and Sixth Centuries

With the close of the fourth century, there is no direct mention of tongues in operation in the church for "almost one thousand years."[51] Although there is no eyewitness report of the practice, it seems from a historical standpoint that the gift was yet in operation on a minimal scale. One of the few theologians of the six century who was noted as a continuationist was Gregory the Great also known as Pope Gregory I (c. 540 – 604). In his Homilies on Mark 16:17 he states that "…there is something to be said of these signs and powers and of a more veiled nature." The Ancient Commentary makes specific reference that in this instance Gregory is asking a specific question "In what sense do believers today speak in tongues and cast out demons?[52] Gregory further opines:

> "The holy church is even now doing spiritually, every day, what she then did through the apostles corporately… And

---

[51] Kelsey, 38.
[52] Thomas C. Oden, *Ancient Commentary on Scripture. New Testament II, Mark.* (Illinois: Intervarsity Press, 1998), p. 252 (See footnote 37).

any believers whatever who henceforth abandon the profanity of the old life, and utter holy mysteries, and rehearse, as best they can, the praise and power of their maker, what are they doing but 'speaking in new tongues?' ...These signs then, beloved, you do if you will."[53]

At a prima facie reading of this homily, it would seem that Gregory is a proponent of the continuationist view of glossolalia. However, Pope Gregory I is noted to believe that the gifts of the spirit are reserved for clergy. He further felt that laity would do better to concentrate on the fruit of the spirit rather than the gifts of the spirit so that they would not become puffed up with pride.[54]

It would seem that Gregory may have either experienced the gifts of the spirit within his own life or been a witness to others who experienced its manifestation and deemed it special and beyond which the common man could handle. It seems probable that errors of this type led to the further decline of

---

[53] *Gregory the Great*, GMI 455; Migne, PL 76:1169
[54] *Saint Gregory the Great*, Available from
http://www.doctorsofthecatholicchurch.com/GG.html
accessed on 23 April 2010.

manifestations of the Spirit with long-reaching effects on future generations.

The Celtic Church

There are many of the position that those of the Celtic church, St. Patrick (384-461 Aa/D.), (i.e., Bede, and others), during this era who experienced gifts of miracles and healings, as well as some reference to speaking in tongues. However, references to original documents by no means reflect such occurrences. In fact, theologians quote St. Patrick to support the position that St. Patrick spoke in tongues as follows:

> "I saw Him [Jesus] praying within me and I was, as it were, inside my own body and I heard His voice above me, that is to say above my inner self, and He was praying there powerfully and groaning; and meanwhile I was dumbfounded and they astonished and wondered who it could be that was praying with me, but at the end of the prayer He spoke and said that He was the Spirit . The Spirit helps the weaknesses of our prayer; for we do not know what to pray for as we ought; but the Spirit Himself intercedes for us with

unspeakable groans which cannot be expressedin words. (Romans 8.26) and again: 'The Lord, our advocate, intercedes for us.' (1 John 2:1)[55]

Indeed, this could be one of the few times through the centuries that bears some credence to the attestation of speaking in tongues after the first century church and one can be surmised that Patrick was not alone in this experience among his contemporaries but that there was likely a sect of believers that experienced the manifestation of speaking in tongues. Conversely, many proponents of Celtic pneumatology credit St. Columba (521-597A.D.) with having the gift of speaking in tongues although there is no written historical evidence to support it.

> "As well as being a political prophet, Columba was, if we are to believe his early biographers, a miracle worker, and faith healer… The only gift of the spirit that he is not portrayed as possessing is that of speaking in tongues."[56]

Although many historians state that the practice of

---

[55] Patrick, *Confession*, Declaration 25

[56] Ian Bradley, *Columba, Pilgrim and Penitent*,(United Kingdom, Wild Goose Publications, 1998), pg. 111

both xenoglossia and glossolalia had essentially ceased during the medieval period, recent study has revealed that this may not be the case. A deep study of this period by Cooper-Rompato sheds new light on the topic and that there were some occurrences of the manifestation during this period .

> "...xenoglossic holy men must be added a number of male saints, including SS. Christopher, Basil the Great, Ephrem, Patiens, Norbert, Andreas Stultus (the Fool for Christ), Francis of Assisi, Teilo, Padarn, David, and Cadoc... list of holy women, St. Lutgard of Aywieres, St. Bridget of Sweden, and the fifteenth-century English mystic Margery Kempe must be included for their gifts of vernacular xenoglossia. When we consider the gift of Latin for holy women as a variation of xenoglossia, the list becomes much longer, including, for example, SS. Catherine of Siena, Elizabeth of Schönau, Bridget of Sweden, Umiltá of Faenza, Blessed Ida of Louvain, and Christina Mirabilis, in addition to a number of other women."[57]

---

[57] Cooper-Rompato, Christine F;. The Gift of Tongues. Women's Xenoglossia in the Later Middle Ages. Penns State University Press 2011, p. 14

St. Padarn (490-550AD) was a native of France who journeyed to the British Isles, and settled in Wales as a monk. It was during his journey to find his father that he decided to live a life devoted to God and prayer. "St Padarn and Teilo.' Soon David sent to them. They came without delay. They passed together through barbarous nations, receiving the gift of tongues. For they were men of one language, and were addressing every man in his **own language, wherein he had been born.** "[58]

Discussion and Reflection Questions

1. In your opinion, how fluent was the fifth century church in understanding the doctrine of being filled with the spirit? How capable is today's average congregation of understanding spiritual matters? How does this affect the church today?
2. What was the understanding of the fifth and sixth century church concerning being filled with the spirit?
3. Does it seem probable that given the example of St. Patrick that there were numerous other individuals that had a spiritual experience other than speaking in tongues? If so, in what way?
4. To what decree did the Pope Gregory appear to accept the spiritual practices of the Christians?

---

[58] Charles Thomas and David R. Howlett, *Vita Sancti Paterni: The Life of Saint Pardarn.* Trivium Publications, 2003

Chapter 5
The Seventh and Eighth Centuries

With the Roman Catholic Church fully established we see man's quest for power, in operation in some of its leaders. Many of the church leaders thought that laity could not understand the things of God and God's Word was reserved for specific understanding solely for clergy. In fact, the church services were held most prominently in Latin and people could not understand the language much less what the teachings of the Bible were all about. The Pope was the Vicar of Christ, and the church had as much authority as the Word of God in the eyes of the Catholic Church.

Many evangelical churches of today would view this as a great apostasy because people were to serve the church and less emphasis was placed on a relationship with God. This may be one of the factors that contributed to the scarcity of gifts of the spirit in operation in the church. As in centuries before, the gifts of the spirit have not totally vanished although, there is very little mention of the activity of speaking in tongues in the seventh century. It may be contended that one author who may be referring to the activity is a monk of the 7th and early eighth century named Saint Bede who states in his Commentary on Jude 20 that:

> "…we pray in the Holy Spirit when we are moved by divine inspiration to ask for heavenly help, so that we may receive the good things which we cannot obtain on our own."[59]

Although he makes mention of divine inspiration to help us in prayer, he does not say outright that the practice of glossolalia in prayer is in operation here. Therefore, it is dubious.

This period of time is the dawning of the middle ages which is noted for very little academic and spiritual enlightening. There is, however, a secondary source which points out minimal ecstatic utterance which has been backed up by a few older sources.

---

[59]Saint Bede, *Ancient Christian Commentary on Scripture: New Testament XI, James, 1-2 Peter, 1-3 John, Jude.* Ed. Gerald Bray and Thomas C. Oden (Illinois: InterVarsity Press, 2000), 257 (Original source in Latin by J..P. Migne, ed. Patrologia Latina.221 vols. Paris Migne 1844-1864), 93:129

> "During the Middle Ages, the incidence of glossolalia is not well known, although, according to biographies (Lombard 1910:106-7), St. Hildegarde is said to have possessed the gift of visions and prophecy and to have been able to speak and write in Latin without having learned the language…"[60]

In the middle ages there are a few brief and obscure references to something that could possibly be glossolalia, however, by and large, there is little to no evidence to support and widespread practice. There are a few theologians that will provide examples of such occasions in an effort to prove the continuity of glossolalia as a viable spiritual experience. However, the few instances that can be referenced may provide the evidence necessary for viability as a matter of faith. The question then becomes, "Is overwhelming continuity of glossolalia in history necessary to prove its feasibility for the Pentecostal experience? Will there be times in history when the operation of the 'spirit' will be greater than at others? "

---

[60] May, L. Carlyle, A Survey of Glossolalia and Related Phenomenon in Non-Christian Religions. American Anthropologist, https://anthrosource.onlinelibrary.wiley.com/doi/pdf/10.1525/aa.1956.58.1.02a00060 retrieved on January 31, 2018

Discussion and Reflection Questions

1. With the Advent of the Dark Ages, why do you think there so little evidence of speaking in tongues in the Middle Ages?
2. Is there a possibility that there were occurrences within certain sects that have been lost to history?
3. Does speaking in tongues make one a greater or better Christian?
4. Do you believe that there is a connection between prayer and glossolalia?

Chapter 6

The Ninth through the Thirteenth Centuries

Notable theologians such as Stanley Burgess found no testimony of the practice of glossolalia during this time which is evidence that its practice was either practiced and not recorded by men and women of obscurity within history or that there was no practice during this time. During these centuries history lets us know that there was a spiritual breakdown of the Catholic Church. There was fighting for power among its bishops and between the kings as to who had the right to choose popes. Islam had taken over the holy city of Jerusalem and there was much bloodshed in the name of God and Christianity to recover the holy city during the Crusades. It seemed as if the spiritual experience was on the back burner while humanity pursued prominence, wealth and status in the world. Spiritual gifts were overshadowed by conquests. Given the turmoil and the bloodshed, God's spirit did not totally disappear from the earth. There is minuscule evidence of glossolalia during this period, but God was still present in the lives of his people. Because of the apostasy of the church, we would agree with the theologian John Wesley as to the reason for the decline in the manifestation of the Holy Spirit over the centuries. Wesley believes that humans fell away from the things of God. God will not force himself upon humans. If people draw away from the spirit, the Holy Spirit is a gentleman and will retreat but will return when he is desired and sought after. Donald Gee drawing from John Wesley states:

> "…there was a great diminution of these gifts not only after the apostolic age, but probably even towards its close…this was not because the Lord withdrew them. Instead, it was because men 'fell away'…Because the love of many, mostso-calledChristianswas waxed cold….This was the real cause why the extraordinary gifts of the Holy Ghost were no longer to be found in the Christian church."[61]

Another possibility is that given there may have been a decline in literacy during this period, and those who practiced this phenomenon were neither inclined

---

[61] Donald Gee, *Concerning Spiritual Gifts*, (Missouri, Gospel Publishing House, n.d.), 11-12.

nor able to record the event. This could be possible if history does repeat itself. Such was the case in the early church. It is well documented that the gospels were not written by the apostles themselves but that they were written by highly literate Greeks at least 30 years after the death of Jesus. The early church primarily relied upon oral history at its inception to tell the story of Jesus. The church became more organized when the oral history was written in the form of the gospels we now have as well as other apocryphal writings. Although this may be the case, it is a fact that there was a great decline of gifts of the spirit in operation in the church during this time.

Some of the few references to glossolalia during this time are associated with heretical movements such as Simeon the New Theologian (949-1022 A.D.) "…an eastern mystic reports his most intimate spiritual experiences, including a 'baptism in the Holy Spirit'…"[62] St Hildegard of Bingen (1098-1179) This is a rare occurrence where we a woman who as noted in history as spoken and sung in tongues. She is noted as singing in tongues as well as having written books in unknown languages. It seems that to haven't been noted in history as a prophetess, her gift would have

---

[62] Burgess, *The Pentecostal Tradition*, 40.

been exceptional and that she was well known. Particularly to have been a woman of the medieval era, she had great influence upon the people. Another point here is that Hildegard was not a Christian as we would use the term today. She was a Benedictine abbess and was dedicated to "a monastic life of obedience and communal pray." [63] Although many regard her as a mystic, she was one who had evangelized and preached the Bible and regarded her relations with Jesus highly. The fact that she preached does not validate her spiritual experiences as authentic or fraudulent. What would be her testimony is an orthodox lifestyle consecrated to God and substantiated by the Holy Spirit, of which the research cannot be the judge.

Thomas Aquinas (1225–1274 A.D.) seems to be a proponent of speaking in tongues. Although he does not state so outright, in Summa Theologica in answer to Question 176 "Whether the gift of tongues is more excellent that than the grace of prophecy", he argues that the gift of prophecy is greater than the gift of speaking in tongues which lets us know that he is a proponent of both the prophetic and glossolalia in the life of the church.

---

[63] Saint Hildegard, *Scivias / Hildegard of Bingen,* (New York, Paulist Press, c.1990), 2.

> "...by the gift of prophecy man is directed to God in his mind, which is more excellent than being directed to Him in his tongue. "He that speaketh in a tongue "is said to speak "not unto men," i.e., to men's understanding or profit, but unto God's understanding and praise. On the other hand, by prophecy a man is directed both to God and to man; wherefore it is the more perfect gift."[64]

Thomas Aquinas use of the word "is" insinuates that both gifts are for the current life of the church. It does not delineate that the gift was active in the past and has ceased. In biblical terms, these few instances support that scriptures and the promise of the spirit abiding during this age would not cease until the future age as prophesied in Joel 2 and confirmed in John 14:16-17.

> "And I will ask the Father, and he will give you another Helper….even the Spirit of truth, whom the world cannot receive, because it neither sees him nor knows him. You know him, for he dwells with you and will be in you."

---

[64] Thomas Aquinas, *Summa Theologica*, available from http://www.ccel.org/ccel/aquinas/summa.SS.iv.SS_Q176.SS_Q176_A2.html?highlight=speak,in,tongues#highlight , accessed on 1March, 2010.

A well-known advocate of glossolalia in the 13th Century was the Moravian Church. They were known for their doctrine on holiness, piousness and a deep devotion to the things of God. John Roche, who was a critic of the Moravians stated that the Moravians "commonly broke into some disconnected Jargon, which they often passed upon the vulgar, 'as the exuberant and resistless Evacuations of the Spirit'."[65]

The Moravians and others like them were often ostracized and looked at as outcasts of the society. This disassociation from mainline society often led to people of like faiths banning together and forming closed communities which would have added to the mystic of their practices and outsiders would have branded them as heretics. These types of actions would soon lead to the chastisement of society and even worse, the Inquisition.

Xenoglossia in the Late Middle Ages

Present scholarship has examined documents that have recently become available which looks at the speaking in tongues (xenoglossia = a person's ability to speak or write in a language acquired by supernatural

---

[65] John Lacy, *A Cry from the Desert* (London: n.p., 1708), 32. Also appears in The Charismatic Movement, 1975, Michael P. Hamilton, 75.

means.) Christine Cooper-Rompato attempts to dispel a myth that people who spoke in tongues during 1300-1500 were scarce occurrences that were far and few between. Cooper-Rompato notes that there were particularly many women who spoke in tongues during this period.

> "…the accounts emphasize the saints' similarities with the apostles and demonstrate the importance of the theme of conversion in hagiographic literature. For medieval vitae, this includes the conversion not only of non-Christians to Christianity but also of Christians to a more penitent lifestyle, or even the "conversion" of a layperson to the joining of a religious order. The xenoglossic experiences …range from male missionary saints, who are engaged in large-scale preaching efforts and who receive the ability to speak the many languages of their listeners…[66]

Osbourne gives much credit to the Greek

---

[66] Cooper-Rompato, Christine F., The Gift of Tongues: Women's Xenoglossia in the Later Middle Ages, (Penn State University Press.) 2010) pg 20

Orthodox Eastern Church monasteries throughout the Middle Ages for keeping the practice alive.[67]

> "…the abbess Hildegard, whose use of unknown tongues is recorded in the *Lingua Ignota*, or missionaries like Vincent Ferrer (1350-1415) or Francis Xavier (1506-1552), who described their miraculous ability to community with various groups as glossolalia." [68]

One little know figure, Andrew Stultus also known as Andrew the fool (886-912ad) lived during the 10th century in Constantinople he was a slob and from earliest time he had a rich and seed love for God is church and scripture, "the righteous man understood and it spirit that the boys wanted to pain and ask he's wished to speak with him in private through the power and the holy Spirit change the boys language do that of Syrian and sat down and talked with him in fluent Syriac. "[69]

---

[67] Osbourne, G.R., Evangelical Dictionary of Theology (Elwell, Walter G., Editor) Baker Books, Grand Rapids, MI, Pg 1102
[68] Ibid at 1102
[69] Nikephoros, life of Andrew the Fool 2:87

Discussion and Reflection Questions

1. What could be the basis of Cooper-Rompato's position that there were many more occurrences of glossolalia than history records?
2. What part does piety play in the belief in glossolalia? How does the medieval church incorporate piety to its practice?
3. Why is mysticism and glossolalia viewed together during this era? What elements do they share?

Chapter 7
The Fourteenth and Fifteenth Centuries

During these centuries as with most of the middle ages, we see very little practice of glossolalia, which leads to the question of why for the continuationist. One theory which may aid in the continuationist's query is the aspect of spiritual apostasy within the church. With the rise of persecution by those who were against anything outside of the Catholic Church, anyone who engaged in any spiritual activity apart from it were at risk of being found out and thus punished and forced to comply with the orders of the Church.

This low point in spirituality in people's lives is reminiscent of the falling away of the people of God the Old Testament. The church of the New Testament also experienced highs and lows in spiritual manifestation. We see that even Jesus was unable to do great works in certain cities because of the unbelief of the people. In like manner in the Old Testament there was what was called the "Deuteronomic Cycle" which the Israelites were in union with God, then fell into apostasy, God was angered and passed judgment, the people repented, and God restored the people. Could the highs and lows of spiritual manifestation within the New Testament be viewed in similarly? It could be possible that when the church and its leaders got away from the things of God that God withdrew his spiritual manifestation although not withdrawing His spirit from His people? This may be plausible because God is holy and cannot have communion with an unsanctified people.

With that said, there is a rare account advocating glossolalia in his day of an archbishop (formerly a monk) in the Eastern Orthodox Church named Saint Gregory Palamas (1296 – 1359 A.D.) who writes:

> "…emphasizes the laying on of hands for receiving the gifts of healing, miracles, foreknowledge, irrefutable wisdom, diverse tongues and interpretation of tongues."[70]

---

[70] Burgess, *The New International Dictionary of Pentecostal and Charismatic Movements*, 1229.

Through the middle ages, there is very little activity of the spirit manifested among his people and theologians theorize that this may be due to the apostasy of the church keeping in mind that during this era the Church was the initiator of indulgences, confessionals, infallibility of the church and popes as the vicars of Christ. This may be just a few of the many views of the continuationist for virtually little account of tongues during these eras.

Discussion and Reflection Questions

1. What controversies are evident surrounding speaking in tongues during this era?

2. What movements supported the practice? Which movements opposed the practice?

3. Why do you suppose schisms may have risen during this time as opposed to other periods?

4. How does a medieval interpretation of the New Testament affect its understanding of spiritual practice?

Chapter 8

The Sixteenth Century: The Protestant Reformation

With the birth of the Protestant Reformation, a spiritual rebirth began to take place; however, we will see that their focus was not that of glossolalia but that of the works of the spirit from the context of grace which had ceased from being manifested within the church.

To get an accurate depiction of the early reformers thoughts on glossolalia, it is again important to turn to the primary sources which in this case would be their commentaries on the occurrences of Pentecost and Paul's First letter to the church of Corinth. First, the examination of the father of reformed theology, John Calvin, on his reflection on Acts two reveals that John Calvin believed that the gift of tongues was poured upon the apostles mainly for two reasons (1) a sign to the unbelievers and (2) that when the apostles spoke the good news of God and Jesus, that men would understand them.[71]

Calvin was further a cessationist stating in his commentary on Acts 10:44-48 that "The gift of the tongues and other such like things are ceased long ago in the church…"[72] He further states in his commentary on I Corinthians 12: 10 that the knowledge and interpretation of tongues was bestowed on those "not acquainted with the langue of the nation with which they had to deal."[73] Calvin's interpretation here reveals his position on xenolalia as a tool for evangelism and detracts from a position of glossolalia as an enabler for preaching with power.

Like Calvin, Luther was also a cessationist. He stated in his treatise Against Andreas Bodenstein von Carlstadt that the gift of tongues was given for a sign to the Jews and that this demonstration is no longer needed in the church. Luther further makes an indirect assertion on 1 Corinthians 14 in which he is against a different language being spoken in church services

---

[71]John Calvin, *Commentary on Acts*. Acts 2:1-4 Available from http://www.ccel.org/ccel/calvin/calcom36.ix.i.html Accessed on 25 March 2010.
[72] Ibid., Acts 10:44-48.
[73] Ibid., I Cor. 12:10

(Latin) and is a proponent of the scripture being spoken in the language which laity can understand. Some researchers misapply this quotation to reflect Luther's advocacy of speaking in tongues in church, but when read in context, he is speaking about Holy Scripture being given in a language that everyone can understand.

> 'Whoever comes forward, and wants to read, teach, or preach, and yet speaks with tongues, that is, speaks Latin instead of German, or some unknown language, he is to be silent and preach to himself alone. For no one can hear it or understand it, and no one can get any benefit from it. Or if he should speak with tongues, he ought, in addition, to put what he says into German, or interpret it in one way or another, so that the congregation may understand it.'

Although Calvin and Luther spoke of the Holy Spirit in their commentaries, they do not associate it with glossolalia. In fact, they do not mention this activity as a viable sign of Christ's presence within the church. Instead, they prominently associate the Holy Spirit with the work of grace within the life of the believer. However, this resurgence in personal faith gave root to other denominations that placed piety and spiritual inspiration at the forefront of their belief system.

Through our journey, we see that speaking in tongues was not a predominant feature within Christian congregations until, the sixteenth century within the offshoots of the Reformation era among the Anabaptists. Thomas Muntzer (1488-1525 BC) was considered one of the radical reformers of the Anabaptists. Anabaptists were believers in experiential salvation. They advocated baptism in the Holy Spirit which included speaking in tongues at their services.

> "...excited by mass hysteria, experienced healings, glossolalia, contortions and other manifestations of a camp-meeting revival."[74]

As Calvinism and Lutheranism spread, so did the Anabaptists throughout Europe as well as North America. Their vast appeal was due in part to experience of the transcendent among the common people without the requirement of socioeconomic

---

[74] George Williams, *The Radical Reformation* (Philadelphia: Westminster Press, 1962), 442.

status or hierarchal achievement within the church. It was a freedom of the spirit which lead to the expansion of charisma in Anabaptists and ultimately to other mainline denominations.

Notably, the Jesuits whose origins reside in Roman Catholicism also experienced the opportunity for the manifestation of the gifts of the spirit in the early 16th century. This fact lets us know that the gifts of the spirit within the church do not discriminate based on denominational affiliation. Intimacy with God is at the forefront of his agenda among people who desire Him and seek after him. Such was the case with Ignatius Loyola (1491-1556), founder of the Society of Jesus (the Jesuits) who also saw visions. Burgess states that he had "the gift of *loquela*, which a few modern scholars associate with today's charismatic phenomenon of sung glossolalia [tongues]."[75]

Discussion and Reflection Questions

1. What was the position of the majority of the reformers on being filled with the spirit? What did that look like?

---

[75] Chris Armstrong, *Timeline of the Spirit Gifted*, Available from http://www.christianitytoday.com/ch/news/2002/oct11.html accessed on 19 April 2010

2. How do you suppose Luther's conviction concerning the move of the spirit transformed his own life?

3. How does knowledge of the Reformation affect your personal spiritual conviction?

4. Compare the Reformation with Charismatic renewal of today. What are the similarities? What are the differences?

Chapter 9

The Seventeenth and Eighteenth Centuries

Within the seventeenth and eighteenth centuries, a return to spiritual intimacy with God emerges. With the pioneering works of the great theologians such as Hus, Luther, Calvin, Zwingli, with their call to personal spiritual responsibility to God, we see a desire for intimacy with God returning. The apostasy of the church of former centuries is overshadowed by excitement among believers to experience with God in a personal way. No longer were people held in the dark as to their personal responsibility concerning the things of God. The message began to spread and within these centuries give rise to great theologians and freedom of spiritual expression.

One notable denomination which experienced the transcendent was the Quakers. Spiritual expressions of gratitude to God were in the domain of laity and the common man. Although many Quakers have a history of speaking in tongues, its founder George Fox (1624) discouraged the activity.[76] This did not stop the exuberance of its followers as they experienced something different and personal as they praised God.

As denominations began to express spiritual freedom so too did the Jansenists, who belonged were a branch of the Roman Catholic Church (1640 - 1801 A.D.). They were "known for their signs and wonders, spiritual dancing, healings, and prophetic utterances. Some reportedly speak in unknown tongues and understand foreign languages in which they are addressed."[77]

John Wesley was also a skeptic of the practice of glossolalia but after prayer, contemplation and eyewitness experience to glossolalia and other gifts of the spirit, conceded to the operation of the gift as he was witness to the occurrence among his parishioners and during revivals. His convictions are noted by Watson E. Mills:

---

[76] Stanley M. Burges, "The Pentecostal Tradition, Christian History: The Rise of Pentecostalism," Christianity Today, "(Issue 58, Vol. XVII, No. 2, 1998), 40-1.
[77] Burgess, *Pentecostal and Charismatic Commentary*, 1230.

> "John Wesley struggled with the issue of the propriety of various charismatic displays and finally decided that glossolalia should be counted neither too significant nor too insignificant."[78]

Further, John Wesley believed that in his current day that not all believers would speak with tongues but that some would although there he testifies that he himself did not claim the gift of speaking with tongues.[79]

The Protestant French Huguenots of the late 17th century were devout Christians who were routinely martyred by Catholics for their eccentric spiritual practices. They were also known as Camisards (French Calvinist Protestants. Their manifestation of spiritual, supernatural gifts is well documented along with their proclivity for speaking in tongues.

> "...There was a singular psychologic or spiritual phase in the history of the Christians. that mustbe noticed. It was a sort of inspiration or ecstasy. The subject

---

[78] Watson E. Mills, *Speaking in Tongues: Let's Talk About It*, (Texas: Word Books, 1973), 78.

[79] John Wesley, *The Works of the Rev. John Wesley in Ten Volumes*, (New York, J. & J. Harper, 1827) Vol. IX, p.73

who had endured longfasting became pale and fell insensible to the ground. Then came violent agitations of the limbs and head; and finally the patient, who might be a little child, a woman, or half-witted person, began to speak in good French of the Huguenot Bible, warning the people to repentance, prophesying the immediate coming of the Lord in judgment, and claiming that these exhortations came directly from the Holy Ghost; after a long discourse the patient returns to his native patois (that is, to his illiterate dialect) with no recollection of what he had been doing or saying.[80]

What is interesting from the Huguenot experience is that this is the same kind of manifestation as the Day of Pentecost where the tongues spoken was that of a known unlearned language as opposed to the examples of the current century in which ecstatic utterance is of a heavenly language not understood by humans.

---

[80] Library of Universal Knowledge, Vol. III, page 352. (From A. D. 1685-1705, again A. D. 1715-1729, also A. D. 1775-1789):

Albeit, from these few examples, it seems that the gift of speaking in tongues was manifested within the congregation which may have led some Christian leaders to state their position on the matter. Thus, the Christian community was a tremendous influence upon the writings of theologians because of the personal spiritual experience of laity. This period of time was known as the Great Awakening. The evangelist George Whitfield and John Edwards also ministered during this time. What happened in these revival meters were that spiritual manifestations of the gifts of the spirit began to take place and the common man's expression of faith was freer than either Wesley or Whitfield had anticipated.

> "The Great Awakening and the two great leaders did have critics. Those who favored a middle course for the awakening were called "New Lights." Some opposed the excess emotionalism in the Great Awakening. They became known as the 'Old Lights.'"[81]

---

[81]Paul R. Dienstberger, *The American Republic: A Nation of Christians*. (2000) Available from http://www.prdienstberger.com/nation/Chap2fga.htm#I.%20The%20Early%20Stirrings Accessed on 22 April 2010.

The spiritual movement of this time was the roots of the evangelical movement that we have today. This was only the beginning of what was to come in the early nineteenth century with the Second Great Awakening and in the late nineteenth century and early twentieth century with the holiness movement and the Azusa Street Revivals.

Quaker Movements

Shakers are an offshoot of Quakerism. The founder of the United Society of Believers in Christ's Second Appearing, ("Shakers") was Mother Ann Lee (1736-1784) She taught that the shaking and trembling were caused by sin being purged from the body by the power of the Holy Spirit, purifying the worshiper. During such episodes they would be entranced with shaking, rolling on the floor and speaking in tongues. Mother Lee was radical in that she was a woman preacher of sorts, a rarity of the day. This sect also believed that mother Lee was the feminine second coming of Christ. Although Mother Lee died in 1784, she is created with the Era of Manifestations ("Mother Ann's Work") in which Shakerism experienced its height in popularity (1837-1850s).

> "According to Shaker tradition, heavenly spirits came to earth, bringing visions, often giving them to young Shaker women, who danced, whirled, spoke in tongues, and interpreted these visions through their drawings and dancing."[82]

Ann Lee was born in England and began her ministry (circa 1760) after receiving training from Jane and James Wardley of the early Quakers (Wardley Society). The movement grew, and she decided to take it to America where she started in 1774 in New York City. She preached and had many new converts. The ministry spread to Indiana, Ohio, Kansas, etc. One cannot deny the possibility that Irwin and Parham could have been witness to this new move and incorporated portions of this theology into their own ministries. It is recorded that this new movement was reported on and the news spread through its preachers that were sent out and through news by the invention of the telegraph machine

---

[82] F.W. Evans. Shakers Compendium of the Origin, History, Principles, Rules and Regulations, Government, and Doctrines. (1859). http://www.passtheword.org/SHAKER-MANUSCRIPTS/Shakers-Compendium/shaker1x.htm Retrieved March 23, 2014.

Discussion and Reflection Questions

1. Do you believe that John Wesley would support the neo-pentecostal movement of the present day?
2. In what ways are Methodism and Pentecostalism similar? How are they different?
3. Would you consider Quakerism a forerunner to Pentecostalism? Why or why not?
4. What was women's influence upon the movement during this time?

Chapter 10
The Nineteenth Century

Within the nineteenth century is recorded an abundance of first-hand witnesses as to the practices of glossolalia on the earth among devout Christians. There is a return among believers to piety and the search of authentic spiritual life of the believer. We see this within the movements of the great revivals the arrival of the Second Great Awakening

During the time of the Second Great Awakening was the rise of the Irvingites which was started by Edward Irving (1792-1842A.D.) who was a minister in the Church of Scotland. Irving recounts an event of a woman who would "speak at great length, and with superhuman strength, in an unknown tongue, to the great astonishment of all who heard, and to her own great edification and enjoyment in God..."[83]

---

[83] Edward Irving, *Facts Connected with Recent Manifestations of Spiritual Gifts*, Fraser's Magazine for Town and Country, Vol. 4), p. 760.

"In these views he [Irving] was greatly strengthened by the sudden reappearance of what he believed to be the supernatural gifts of tongues, prophesying, and healing. ...They united in supplications for the restoration of spiritual gifts. In April 1831, the same manifestations took place among members of the Church of England and friends of Irving in London. The 'prophesying' was addressed to the audience in intelligible English and resembled the solemn exhortations of Quakers moved by the Spirit. The speaking in tongues consisted of soliloquies of the speaker, or dialogues between him and God which no one could understand... " [84]

Within the Catholic Church (circa 1830) little-known manifestations tongues occurred within the

---

[84] Paul Schaeff, *Creeds of Christendom with a History and Critical Notes, Volume I, The History of Creeds,* The Catholic Apostolic Church (called Irvingites) §113. Available from http://www.ccel.org/ccel/schaff/creeds1.html accessed on 20 April, 2010.

Catholic Apostolic Church under the leadership of Edward Irving. The movement was coined as "Irvingism," and there is evidenced that they experienced a revival speaking in tongues as early as the last quarter of the 18th century.[85]

Specific reference is given in a letter of Irving of 1831 where he mentions quote two of my flock have received the gift of tongues and prophecy.[86]

Further, speaking in tongues may have received acclamation as the first movement for speaking in tongues, but in fact, there was also a movement in 1855 and continuing which Parham may have had knowledge of as an itinerant preacher. William H. Doughtery of Rhode Island is reported to have spoken in tongues predating the Topeka Kansas experience by as much as three decades.

"...In the year 1875 our Lord began to pour upon us His Spirit; and wife and I, with a few others, began to utter a few words in the unknown tongue...While we were seeking the baptism, there came among us several who had received the baptism and the gift of tongues a number of years before this...they are now sleeping in

---

[85] Synan, Vinson, *Aspects of Pentecostal Charismatic Origins*, Logos International, Plainfield New Jersey 1975 page 17
[86] .Ibid at 19

Jesus ...their names follow...Wm. H. Doughty of Maine, Amanda Doughty...Zina Ford of Concord, N.H., Wm. Hawkes of East Boston, Mass., Eliza Libby of Lawrence Mass, Rose Jenkins of Vermont, Rosa Childs of Hartford, Conn... "[87]

The movement spread through Scotland and England and it's further recorded that on April 30th, 1831 the first manifestation took place in London misses John Cardiel, wife of a prominent Anglican lawyer, spoke in tongues. Edward Drummond records that "...during the course of that year, tongues and prophecy were experienced by several other persons from various religious denominations."[88]

Not only were manifestations evident in Europe but also in Canada. In 1857 phone Palmer, a Methodist evangelist, reports that during camp revivals many received the baptism of fire (Holy Ghost). Palmer, Phoebe, Beauty of holiness, 8 June 1857, 164-5

There is no question that within the 19th century

---

[87] Lawrence, B.F. "A History of the Present Latter Rain Outpouring of the Holy Spirit Known as the Apostolic or Pentecostal Movement," The Weekly Evangel, 22 January 1916. http://enrichmentjournal.ag.org/200602/200602_078_AzusaDoctrine_84_RI.cfm

[88] "Drummond, Edward, *Irving and His Circle*, London, James Clark & Company, 1934, page 153

there was a reemergence of interest in the experience of speaking in tongues which had long leg dormant. The root emphasis of spiritual expression was wedged predominantly in the First and Second Great Awakenings of the Methodist movement (John Wesley and George Whitfield) and spread worldwide.

Although the Azusa Street Revival is credited with the reemergence of speaking in tongues in the United States, there were several forerunners from which both Parham and Seymour may have borrowed their Theology of speaking in tongues. One of note is Abner Blackman Crumpler who was a Methodist Holiness preacher rooted in North Carolina, and he is credited with the Pentecostal Holiness Church but having been founded in 1898. Another was Benjamin H Irwin (1854-) who was a former Baptist preacher from Iowa who was the founder of the Fire Baptized Holiness Church in Anderson, South Carolina. This is evidence that there was something coming to light with regard to speaking in tongues in the early 20th century and that the credit of the doctrine of speaking in tongues may not have originated with Charles Parham as has been credited in earlier works. It is highly likely that in these circles that these holy men converged and shared ideas given that they were from the same general time. Further many of them had Southern boots, and the fire was spreading prior to 1906. Azusa Street Revival can be credited with the spread nation and World Wide of the emergence of tongues. However its origins or deeply rooted in the Bible Belt.

In fact, Ken Sumrall believed most of the ministers of the church had received the baptism of the Holy Spirit with evidence by speaking in tongues. They had embraced the teaching of GB Cashwell, who was a witness to the Azusa Street revival of 1906. In 1908, the church "...changed its doctrine to embrace the Pentecostal view of times..."[89] and thereby they became the first official Pentecostal denomination in the United States. In 1911 the Fire-Baptized Holiness Church (ibid)

During this outburst, most notably we have the occurrences of Charles Parham and William Seymour. Parham. Parham was a holiness preacher in Topeka Kansas during the late 1800 who was the teacher of William Seymour for about three months.

Parham's first exposure to the Holiness movement was through his wife Cyrus's Wings whose father was a circuit preacher stemming from Quakerism. Through this was his Genesis of the Pentecostal experience. It

---

[89]Shiver, Terry. D., *Ken Sumrall and Church Foundation Network: A Modern-day Apostolic Movement.* Wipf &stock publishers 2015

The History of Speaking in Tongues

has been suggested that his theology evolve.Over time, however, his Doctrine appears to have existed early on, and so much as speaking in tongues is recorded to have happened in his church while he was getting in his twenties. This suggests that he was taught this Dogma early on in his ministry. In fact, the Assemblies of God knew early on that Parham had been exposed to glossolalia prior to his initial evidence theology which preaching in different states.

> "...Given the above accounts, there is some debate as to whether Parham first heard speaking in tongues while at Sandford's Shiloh in Maine or while he was among Fire-Baptized enthusiasts."[90]

Parham's theology also gained new direction through the radical holiness teaching of Benjamin Hardin Irwin and Frank W. Sandford's belief that God would restore xenolalic tongues (i.e., known languages) in the church for missionary evangelism (Acts 2). Along with his students in January 1901, Parham prayed to receive this baptism in the Holy Spirit (a work of grace separate from conversion).[91] In the ensuing revival,

---

[90] Ibid, Hunter
[91] We must note that Parham's initial theology on the purpose of speaking in tongues was that believers would

Parham and many of the students reported being baptized in the Spirit, thus forming an elite band of end time missionaries Parham did not receive the acclaim that Seymour. Many would say that it was due to character flaws and changing religious views. Parham is noted to have been a racist and would not let William Seymour (who was Black) sit in his Bible classes because of his color but would let him sit outside the window of his class so he could hear what was going on. Seymour went on to start the Azusa Street revivals in Los Angeles in 1906 which put glossolalia and the holiness movement on a world stage. Parham's discriminating character was also revealed during the Azusa Street meetings.

> "...Parham arrived in Los Angeles [Azusa Street Revival] and was horrified to see the informality of black-white relations there, and especially the contact between black men and white women."[92]

---

speak in known languages "not spirit language" and that xenolalia was to be used as an evangelistic tool. Since their attempt in missions had failed in this wise, glossolalia morphed into a vehicle of an empowered prayer life. (Anderson, Robert Mapes "Vision of the Disinherited: The Making of American Pentecostalism, p. 90)

[92] Apostolic Faith Newsletter, *The Apostolic Faith* (Los Angeles) Vol. 1, no 1 (September 1906), 1-2,4.

It seems as if Parham's character and reputation was his great downfall and God used what would seem foolishness to men as a vehicle to usher in a new wave of spiritual expression in North America. Who would have thought that one of the world's largest denominations would be led by an uneducated and disadvantage man who was the son of ex-slaves? Although Seymour was the least likely candidate as a Christian theologian, Seymour as did the Alexandrian philosopher, Ammonius (440-520 A.D.) agreed that speaking in tongues was evidence that the Holy Spirit had come upon an individual. Ammonius comments on Acts 19:6 stating:

> "...Even if Apollos burned with the Spirit, it is not said that he possessed the Holy Spirit. In fact, he neither was speaking in tongues nor prophesying. Therefore it is one thing to burn with the Spirit and another to possess the Holy Spirit. Whoever possessed the Holy Spirit had it dwelling within him, and the Spirit itself spoke from within."[93]

Although this spiritual awaking had many

---

[93] Ammonius, *Catena on the Acts of the Apostles* 19.5

positive aspects, there was also a failure which is seldom spoken of in the Pentecostal circles. It seems that some of the followers believed that they could go to foreign countries where they would be enabled by the Holy Ghost and the practice of xenolalia to evangelize those who spoke a different language. This misfortune had missionaries coming back to the United States in failure as people of foreign languages were not able to understand the unintelligible speech of these evangelists. This failure, however, did not stop Pentecostalism from spreading on a global scale. The charisma of this movement was undeniable and had vast appeal. People everywhere wanted to experience the transcendent, and this desire continues to this present day. This experience was not limited to the United States. This charismatic movement spread worldwide to places such as Travancore, Scotland, Indonesia, Africa and many other places.

Discussion and Reflection Questions

1. How do you think hierarchy and power within the church adversely affect spiritual matters?
2. Do you think that man's quest for power adversely affects what the spirit wants to do on the earth today?

Chapter 11
Twentieth Century through the Present

According to scholar Vinson Synan, the first record of speaking in tongues during the or of the 20th century is by a woman named Agnes Osmond who spoke in tongues on January 1st, 1901. She was a student of holiness preacher, Charles Fox Parham of the small Bible School in Topeka Kansas. This initiation was, in fact, the first the Pentecostal experience of the 20th century. Synan records:

> "I laid my hands upon her and prayed, Parham later recalled of the event. I scared scarcely competed three dozen sentences when Glory fell upon her, a Halo seemed to surround her head and face, and she began speaking the Chinese language and was unable to speak English for 3 days."[94]

Besides the Holiness Movement, The Great

---

[94] Synan, Vinson, The Century of the Holy Spirit ,Thomas Nelson publishing (Nashville 2001), page 1

Revivals of Wales also influenced the Azusa Street Revivals of 1906. In 1901 The Great Revival of Wales was a precursor to the Azusa Street Revivals. In Wales, they experienced a renewal of the presence of God,but the Azusa Street Revival was different because here they experienced the most notable experience glossolalia since the early church. The added element of glossolalia had its roots in the holiness movement of the late nineteenth and early 20th century and its far-reachingaffects continued through the twentieth century to the present.

Of note was the experience of Bishop C.H. Mason, founder of the Church of God in Christ who tells of his experience of being baptized in the Holy Ghost during the Azusa Street revival.

> "I began to thank God in my heart for all things, for when I heard some speak in tongues, I knew it was right though I did not understand it. Nevertheless, it was sweet to me.
>
> I also thank God for Elder Seymour who came and preached a wonderful sermon...I got a place at the altar and began to thank God. After that, I said Lord if I could only baptize myself, I would do so; for I wanted the baptism so

bad I did not know what to do. I said, Lord, You will have to do the work for me; so I turned it over into His hands

"Then, I began to ask for the baptism of the Holy Ghost according to Acts 2:41, which readeth thus: 'Then I gave up for the Lord to have His way within me. So there came a wave of Glory into me, and all of my beingwas filled with the Glory of the Lord. ."[95]

Pentecostals and Charismatics both believe that glossolalia is for the church today. The point they differ on is that Pentecostals believe that all must speak in tongues to truly belong to the family of God as opposed to the charismatic who believe that the filling of the Holy Spirit does not mean that they will speak in tongues. The New International Dictionary of Pentecostal and Charismatic movements states the differences as follows:'

> "The theological differentiation ... [is] concerning Spirit baptism... which is evidenced by glossolalia; for some this baptism must also follow another act of grace, namely sanctification. Charismatics, on the

---

[95] COGIC History; Bishop C.H. Masson,
http://www.cogic.org/blog/cogic-history-bishop-c-h-mason/

other hand, do not always advocate either the necessity of a second work of grace or the evidence of glossolalia as an affirmation of Spirit baptism. Yet both emphasize the present work of the Spirit through gifts in the life of the individual and the church."[96]

This was a primary doctrine in the Azusa Street Revival which was adopted early on by many Pentecostal denominations. However, years later, Seymour moved away from this tenet and said that spirit baptism is evidenced by the love that believers display.

> "The doctrinal change that resulted is most critical to Pentecostal believers. Seymour moved away from tongues as the initial physical evidence and began to teach that love was the first and major evidence of Spirit baptism. While he did not reject tongues, he did reject the Pentecostal distinctive he had learned under Charles Parham while attending the Apostolic Faith Bible School in Houston, Texas. He apparently held to this altered doctrinal position for the rest of his

---

[96] Stanley M. Burgess, *The New International Dictionary of Pentecostal and Charismatic Movements* (Michigan: Zondervan, 2002), xviii.

ministry."[97]

"As the movement gained experience and moved towards maturity, questions arose that made it more difficult for Seymour to maintain Parham's position...Seymour questioned the legitimacy of tongues as evidence...He believe[d] that baptism with the Spirit was not obtained independently of sanctification, bur rather, as a gift of power on the sanctified life. That meant that while the ability to speak in tongues might signify or act as a sign that followed baptism with the Spirit, other factors had to be weighed which, in Seymour's analysis, proved to be far more important as genuine evidences of the Sprit's baptism."[98]

The research bears out that glossolalia was and is a worldwide practice in the church. Because of distance and more importantly, language barriers it can prove challenging to gain access to primary sources.

---

[97] Hunter, Harold D., *A Portrait of How the Azusa Doctrine of Spirit Baptism Shaped American Pentecostalism*, Enrichment Journal, Assemblies of God.
http://enrichmentjournal.ag.org/200602/200602_078_azusadoctrine.cfm

[98] McGee, Gary B., (Editor) *Initial Evidence: Historical and Biblical Perspective on the Pentecostal Doctrine of Spirit Baptism*, Wipf & Stock Pub(Eugene Oregon 2008),; Robeck, Cecil M., *William J. Seymour ad "The Bible Evidence"* pg. 88

With that in mind, Burgess states that glossolalia is not confined to western Christianity but is recgonized in almost every continent, including Africa:

> "These neocharismatic African churches general accept and practice faith healing, prophetic visions, fervent ecstatic prayer ,and glossolalia...."[99]

The second wave dates from approximately 1960 to 1970s known as the Charismatic movement which is an offspring Pentecostalism and the Azusa Street revivals of 1906. Charismatic is a word combination originally from the Greek *charis* which is the English transliteration of the Greek word for "grace," and *mata*, which is the Greek word meaning "gifts." It is an interdenominational Christian spiritual renewal movement and is set apart from other denominations as it believes in inspiration by the Holy Spirit with frequent expressions of speaking in tongues, shouting, healings, miracles, etc. and is one of the most popular and fastest-growing associations within the Christendom today.[100]

---

[99] Ibid., xx.
[100] Pentecostalism has become the fastest growing family of world Christianity. It is growing at a rate of 13 million a year, or 35,000 a day. With nearly a half billion adherents, it is, after Roman Catholicism, the largest Christian tradition. Christianity Today, "The Rise of Pentecostalism" Issue 58

The term Third wave came into circulation during the 1980s and 1990s. C. Peter Wagner of Fuller Theological Seminary used the phrase to describe Christians who were experiencing the signs and wonders" of the charismatic gifts (including healing, prophecy and speaking in tongues) but were not affiliated with "classical Pentecostal" congregations (dating from the early 1900s) nor linked to the Charismatic Renewal of the 1960s and 1970s in the mainline Protestant Churches and Roman Catholic Church. Third Wave Christians did not think of themselves as Pentecostals or Charismatics, and did not generally accept the "initial evidence" doctrine that speaking in tongues is the necessary outward sign of receiving the "baptism in the Holy Spirit."[101]

Counters to Pentecostalism

Within the present day, there are many proponents of speaking in tongues and the Pentecostal church has gained worldwide acclaim boasting over one million believers that speaking in tongues is a present day reality. This fire has spread even within the portions of Roman Catholic Church who testifies of the

---

[101] McClymond, Michael (Ed.), *Encyclopedia of Religious Revivals in America, Volume Two: Primary Documents* (Connecticut: Greenwood Press, 2007) 348. Cited from Kevin Springer, ed., Power Encounters (1988), set in the 1970s-1980s.

validity of speaking in tongues within their churches.

However, there is a small sect that is gaining speed from the early 1990s and continuing presently whose leader is John MacArthur founder of the "Strange Fire" movement. He purports along with other Christian leaders such as R. C. Sproul, Steve Lawson, Conrad Mbewe, Tom Pennington, Phil Johnson, Nathan Busenitz, Justin Peters, Todd Friel, and Joni Eareckson Tada that speaking in tongues is a heretical practice.

MacArthur views are clear and he states:.

> "...Endless human experiences, emotional experiences, bizarre experiences and demonic experiences are said to come from the Holy Spirit…visions, revelations, voices from heaven, messages from the Spirit through transcendental means, dreams, *speaking in tongues*, prophecies, out of body experiences, trips to heaven, anointings, miracles. All false, all lies, all deceptions attributed falsely to the Holy Spirit . . ..the Charismatic Movement has stolen the Holy Spirit and created a golden calf and they're

dancing around the golden calf as if it were the Holy Spirit.[102]

There are a diversity of evangelical pastors who sit on opposing sides of the debate as whether speaking tongues is a practice in modern church.

Pentecostalism is worldwide. What started out as a denomination made up mostly of uneducated, poor, minorities and disrespected church folks have sparked a light of spiritual passion that cannot be denied regardless of preferred dogma and theological acumen.

We cannot deny that something enlightening happened. And while the denominational leaders may not have fully understood what was happening and the direction to take with the phenomena, it is clear that the spirit filled life has taken a turn to which there is no return. In fact, many denominational rifts and splits occurred early on due to clergies" differences of interpretation of the first wave and the age-old vice of struggles over power.

Discussion and Reflection Questions

1. How do you account for the extreme denominational diversity in neo-pentecostal era?

---

[102] MacArthur, John, Why are evangelicals silent about charismatic error?
https://www.youtube.com/watch?time_continue=4&v=wReegWsBt3M

How does this affect ones spiritual understanding in today's church?
2. Discuss some of the beliefs that charismatics and Pentecostals have in common? What connection do theses denominations have in common with other denominations with the sanctification of man?
3. Point out some of the problems scholars face when trying to compile a history of speaking in tongues?
4. How important were women to cause of continuance of the practice? How valid would their testimony be in a patriarchal society both then and now?
5. Could new archeological finds on the matter sway your doctrinal position?

Conclusion

A survey of glossolalia reveals that the gift is as a tide that ebbs and flows. During some centuries we see a high tide of manifestations, and at other times there is a low tide. The gift was never extinct as some suppose. There seems to have always been a remnant, no matter how large or small of those that felt the wave of the spirit with a manifestation of either xenolalia or glossolalia. This testimony is evident not only within specific denominations but was broader. People of numerous denominations felt this wave and engaged in oneness with the spirit of God

Speaking in tongues as a Christian practice was unseen before the Day of Pentecost. However, a heretical form of ecstasy was extant prior thereto in pagan religions including after the day of Pentecost in many heretical movements. The Catholic viewpoint states that "it [glossolalia] is found in almost all religious traditions, particularly in primitive forms of worship and especially as a group phenomenon."[103] While many pagan religions practice ecstatic utterance, the Christian experience of glossolalia is different from the pagan and heretical practices.

First, there is nothing like the experience of glossolalia that can be compared to that which took place on the Day of Pentecost. Kelsey confirms this by letting us know the nuances of ecstatic speech in paganism because of the obscurity of their practices as well as the use of a "trance medium" in many cases.[104] Further, the Old Testament parallels are equally denied because the Old Testament examples "show little relationship to the experience of tongues as described by Paul or Luke in the Book of Acts."[105]

Accordingly, glossolalia experienced by those of the Day of Pentecost was unique and authentic to the orthodoxy of the early church. If the Bible is, in fact, inerrant then the practice of glossolalia as practiced in the early church is indeed for the church today as stated in John 14:16 " And I will ask the Father, and he will gift you another Counselor to be with you forever."

---

[103] Richard P. McBrien, Harld W. Attridge, *The Harper Collins Encyclopedia of Catholicism* (California: HarperSanFranciso, 1995), 562.
[104] Kelsey, ibid, 140
[105] Kelsey, Ibid, 141

Through this journey, we have seen that glossolalia was in practice from the Day of Pentecost until the present day. Although there were times that the gift was shadowed and hidden from view, God's promise that the gift would be extant until the end of the age was yet in force.

We see also that although the demonic forces have sought to profane and confuse the gift with that of some heterodox practices, God has allowed his gift to remain in the Church. When the believers returned to the pure worship of God and cast aside the seven deadly sins, then we see a church that has repented from apostasy and God returns to loving intimacy with His people.

One cannot deny that glossolalia is based upon personal experience. The importance of personal experience in the life of the church as it pertains to doctrine has long been debated. Paul notes the gift of tongues as an aspect of personal experience in I Cor. 14:4 in that its practice "edifies himself. He builds upon his own faith and spiritual life by being in direct communion with God by the Spirit which bypasses his own understanding.

This personal experience is present for the Holy Spirit helps us to pray. Paul states that "the Spirit also helpeth our infirmity: for we know not how to pray as we ought, but the Spirit himself maketh intercession for us with groanings which cannot be uttered" (Rom. 8:26). Through glossolalia, God helps mere humans to communicate with him. Tongues take the present day believer and transcends understanding to the very presence of God. Paul states that "For anyone who speaks in a tongue does not speak to men but to God. Indeed no one understands him; he utters mysteries with his spirit." (1 Co. 14:1-2). Believers do this in prayer praise and thanksgiving wherein he is strengthened and edified by the very presence of God.

The Holy Spirit (parakletoς) the one who walks alongside us and is our advocate continues to this very day and throughout this age to help the devout followers of Christ to communicate with God. This is God's very presence abiding with us in a powerful way.

> "Or know ye not that your body is the temple of the Holy Spirit which is in you, which ye have from God? and ye are not your own; for ye were bought with a price: glorify God therefore in your body" (1 Cor. 6:19).

As to the debate on other tongues versus heavenly tongues referred to in 1 Co. 14, Timothy Luke Johnson makes this observation:

> "Paul clearly regards tongues as unintelligible, contrasting speech that is "in the Spirit (en to pneumati) but does not use the mind (nous), with speech that does use the mind and therefore builds up the community. (1Cor 14:14-15, 19). Because glossolalia is a private and non-communicative, God may be praised by it and the person praying may be edified but neither the mind or the community gain any benefit from the performance. (1 Cor. 14:2-3, 14, 17, 28).[106]

Johnson provides evidence that Paul was referring to the heavenly language concerning the use of tongues as personal edification which is widely practiced in the new wave of Pentecostalism. This practice is not a new contrivance for Christians but is merely a return to the initial purpose of the Holy Ghost in the life of believers. As with the church of Corinth, today believers must guard against two things. First, that the gift is manifested in appropriate settings. Paul admonishes the

---

[106] Johnaon, Luke Timothy, *Religious Experience in the earliest Christianity: A Missing Dimension in New Testament Studies*, (Minnesota: Augsburg Fortress, 1998), 113.

Church of Corinth that they have control over their bodies and how the gift is manifested in the midst of the congregation. He states that if they are going to speak loudly in the congregations for others to hear then interpretation must follow. Thus the inference is that if you are speaking in tongues for self-edification then speaking in tongues should be practiced in private devotion or very lowly at appropriate times in during church gatherings.

Second, the Pentecostal should have balance within their spiritual lives. The church of Corinth's desire to speak in tongues was predominant and great value was placed on possessing this gift as opposed to the other spiritual gifts, but Paul tries to bring balance in highlighting the other gifts to let them know that all the gifts are important to the health of the church.

Some denominations have placed a heavy emphasis on speaking in tongues, to the point where they teach that if you do not speak in tongues, there you don't have Christ in your heart. Evangelist David Wilkerson is of the opinion, (and I tend to agree) that some have gone "overboard" on tongues and said that some preachers preach tongues more than they preach Christ. Wilkerson teaches that "true Holy Ghost baptism is a baptism of love that helps you see and love a lost world through the eyes of Jesus....I speak with tongues in my secret closet of prayer...It is not a group or public experience. No one else is involved but Jesus and me.!"[107]

Lastly, not all believers will speak in tongues. Paul clearly points out that the body of Christ in one but with many parts. (1 Cor 12:12ff). There are different manifestations of the gifts of the spirit and God may have gifted us in something other than the gift of tongues. Therefore, the place of glossolalia within the local assembly should be tempered by the precepts of God's Word. The focus of the local assembly should focus more on the fruit of the spirit for in Paul's admonition he reflects on the importance of love, which also points to the Golden Rule of loving God and loving your neighbor as yourself. For if you speak with tongues and don't' love, it means absolutely nothing (1 Co. 13:1ff).

It was suspected by many by the close of the Azusa Street Revivals that speaking in tongues was a wonderful gift, but that it was not primary evidence of being filled with the Holy Spirit. Ms. Ozman, who was has been noted as the first speak in tongues under

---

[107]David Wilkerson Speaks Out, Brooklyn, N.Y.; Teen Challenge Publications, June 1972, pg 4-5

Parham in Topeka Kansas as well as her claim to have written in Chinese without any knowledge or education to that effect which proved to be erroneous and nonsensical. Below is the actual writing of Ozman's claimed Chinese writing.

Ozman proclaimed that this was the evidence of being baptized with the holy spirit but later pulled back from the initial evidence theory in stating that the revivalists were in danger of walking in error concerning this issue. In fact, as early as 1909 she was attempting to bring correction on this very matter, but her words fell on deaf ears and as a result, there are various denominations and millions of people that have been taught that speaking in tongues is the sole evidence of being filled with the Holy Spirit. These denominations preach that if you don't speak in tongues, then you don't have the holy spirit and that you don't belong to Christ even though you have repented of your sins and made

Jesus lord of your life. Ms. Ozman and other early Pentecostals echo the sentiment that this is error.

> "...Later in her life Agnes admitted that she had been wrong to believe that all people would speak in tongues when they were baptized with the Holy Spirit. Writing in The Latter Rain Evangel of January 1909 she wrote, 'Some time ago I tried but failed to have an article printed which I wrote calling attention to what I am sure God showed me was error. The article maintained that tongues was not the only evidence of the Spirit's Baptism. When that article was refused I was much tempted by Satan, but God again graciously showed me He had revealed it to me, and satisfied my heart in praying that He might reveal this truth to others who would spread it abroad. For awhile after the baptism I got into spiritual darkness, because I did as I see so many others are doing these days, rested and reveled in tongues and other demonstrations instead of resting alone in God.'"[108]

---

[108] Ozman-LaBarge, Agnes "When The Latter Rain First Fell: The First One to Speak in Tongues". In The Latter Rain Evangel, January 1909, p.2. Available online at http://pentecostalarchives.org/digitalPublications/USA/Independent/Latter%20Rain%20Evangel/Unregistered/1909/FPHC/1909_01.pdf

This early deviation from the founding doctrine beginning with Charles Parham is a pivotal point of the evolution of speaking in tongues as a mandate for salvation to the second wave of charismatic renewal of speaking in tongues as a gift and aid in prayer. Ms. Ozman sums up the importance resting in and loving God as the standard of salvation. One cannot help but to reminisce on the words of Paul where he states:

> [4] But God, being rich in mercy, because of His great love with which He loved us, [5] even when we were dead [f] in our transgressions, made us alive together [g] with Christ (by **grace you have been saved**), [6] and raised us up with Him, and seated us with Him in the heavenly *places* in Christ Jesus, [7] so that in the ages to come He might show the surpassing riches of His grace in kindness toward us in Christ Jesus. [8] **For by grace you have been saved through faith;** and that not of yourselves, *it is* the gift of God; [9] not as a result of works, so that no one may boast. [10] For we are His workmanship, created in Christ Jesus for good works, which God prepared beforehand so that we would walk in them. (Eph. 8:4-10)

Salvation is God's gift to humankind. The Holy Spirit is God's gift to us. Speaking in tongues is His gift to us. How he manifests and when he manifests these graces of His spirit is His decision alone. Many look for more of God through filling of the holy spirit but God's spirit is in and with us as a work of grace and people who may not have yet received the gift of speaking in tongues should feel no less a Christian or as God's step child because of it. He loves all His children and has a work in mind for all in accordance with His will. God gives as and when He sees fit. The aspect of the love of God and the love of your neighbor is unique to the Christian experience of glossolalia. Although ecstatic utterance predates and is profaned within modern times, love remains a feature to be incorporated with the gift, and that is unique and authentic.

The Fourth wave of the Pentecostalism/Charismatic experience is upon us today and is filled with individuals who want to not only go to church but want to experience God. Although there is a strong relational desire for spirituality, today's tech savvy and social media millennial desires are ultra inquisitive and are not afraid to ask the hard questions about in reference thereto. They have faith but are acutely aware of other worldviews and will consider them in their own spiritual journey. We find their vocations in all walks of life and melding together their faith in all arenas.

This Fourth Wave emphasizes societal change by channeling these empowered believers to impact the seven cultural mounts of religion, government, education, business, family, media and the arts and entertainment. Fresh intercessory strategies will now arise for effective ministry in the marketplace. The supernatural power of the Holy Spirit will not be able to be contained within the "four walls of the church" but rather explode into every sphere of life.[109]

Where to We Go From Here?

Speaking in tongues will continue to be a debated issue for many years to come, but some good has come from the Pentecostal movement of the 20th century to the present and though many would disagree with its practice, there has been much good that has come from it. Let's consider the good that J.I. Packer points out.[110]

---

[109] Goll, Dr. James, The Fourth Great Wave of the Holy Spirit https://www.charismanews.com/opinion/56670-the-fourth-great-wave-of-the-holy-spirit-has-begun
[110] Packer, J. I. *Keep in Step with the Spirit*. IVP, 1984, p. 183-197.

As to the spirit, we have been pointed towards being dependent upon Christ and the supernatural to work in the life of the believer. The first Pentecostals relied heavily on the spirit leading in all aspects of life. True there was a misunderstanding in many ways of the way in which God was moving. But the accomplishment of a deeper spirituality was indeed achieved.

Further, as a result of the inward manifestation of the spirit within us, believers are pointed towards active engagement and a deeper relationship with Christ. The end result is engagement with God through joyfulness, prayerfulness and worshipfulness which deals with man's attitudes towards God's saving grace and being in relationship with God as opposed to a life of religiosity and the doing of good works as a duty.

Man's active interaction with the Divine empowers believers to do more than just exist. It propels believers to live a life that is transcendent of negative impulses and selfishness to rise above the human condition.

The good seems to outweigh the bad in that it has caused a spiritual stirring in the earth that may not have otherwise happened. Dry and cold religious experience lacked the spontaneity, drive and passion needed to reach a dying world. Christ said that the foolish things will confound the wise. Indeed glossolalia could be considered as such. To the learned, it doesn't make sense. It is misunderstood and debated repeatedly within the highest scholarly circles. But experience with the very presence of something beyond who you are right now calls us to our better self.

As to the continuity of the practice of speaking in tongues, we can say that as with anything else, you cannot always remain on a spiritual high and you will not always remain at a low--so it is with speaking in tongues through the centuries. There are times when it seems that as if speaking in tongues as a full-blown wave and then there are times when speaking in tongues is but a small way that ebbs and flows with time and as the spirit sees fit to intervene and show up in mighty ways in the affairs of man.

Indeed Pentecostalism renewed and set the stage for a revived Church and through which God reinvigorated His people to do great exploits such as the world has never seen before. Whether proponent or foe one cannot deny the expanse of the Gospel through Pentecostalism. It is a fact.

As with anything that God does the enemy will always try to exploit and pervert and caused many to go astray so that they will not believe that the power that they see is actually from God and sanctions by the holy Spirit. Fanaticism frightens and drives away many possible converts and steals the joy that so many could experience have they only believed. It is true that erroneous doctrines are many but such was in the time of the early church as well. We to experience erroneous doctrines but we must always go back to the Bible because the Bible says that in the end days that he would pour out his Spirit upon his people. Why scholars cannot send to embrace this simple truth which God gave us for our benefit is part of the problem within Christianity today.

We must come to God with childlike faith and believe that what he says is true and the stand up on that truth without doubt.

Does this mean that believers will possess the gifts of the spirit, including tongues within society at large? Times are changing. Perspectives and interpretations evolve in hindsight and with the passing of time. Just as a speculator looks at the trends for what stocks to invest in, the church also can speculate what moves God will make in the wave that is upon us. But none can know for certain. We have to be opened to a new and fresh move of God whatever that may entail. We do know that whatever means, the desired end result is the same and that is, that people come to the saving knowledge of God and enter a personal relationship with Him. Like the first wave, they could not tell how that would play out. The Church must be ready for what this entails. Those who are sensitive to what God is doing will be able to flow in whatever move God releases in the earth.

BIBLIOGRAPHY

Aeschylus, *Prometheus Bound*, Claridon Press, Oxford Press, London 1907 p.29 available from

Ammonius, *Catena on the Acts of the Apostles* 19.5.

Apostolic Faith Newsletter, *The Apostolic Faith* (Los Angeles) Vol. 1, no 1 (September 1906), 1-2,4.

Aquinas, Thomas, *Summa Theologica*, Art. 1., Available from,<http://www.ccel.org/ccel/aquinas/summa.SS.iv.SS_Q176.SS_Q176_A1.html?highlight=augustine,tract,xxxii,in,joan,speaks,the,languages#highlight>

Armstrong, Chris, *Timeline of the Spirit Gifted*, Available from <http://www.christianitytoday.com/ch/news/2002/oct11.html>

Augustine of Hippo, *The Gospel of John*, Tractate 32

Augustine of Hippo, *Trinity 15*.

Bale, James D., *Pentecostalism In the Church*, Louisiana, Lambert Book House, 1972

Bromiley, Geoffrey William, *The Encyclopedia of Christianity*, Vol. 2. Michigan: Wm. B. Eerdmans Publishing Co., 2001.

Burgess, Stanley M. Burgess, Eduard M. van der Maas, Ed van der Maas, *The New International Dictionary of Pentecostal and Charismatic Movements*. Michigan, Zondervan, 2002.

Burgess, Stanley M., "The Pentecostal Tradition, Christian History: The Rise of Pentecostalism," *Christianity Today*, (Issue 58, Vol. XVII, No. 2, 1998), 40-1.

Calvin, John, *Commentary on Acts*. Acts 2:1-4, Available from http://www.ccel.org/ccel/calvin/calcom36.ix.i.html,.

Carson, D.A., R.T. France, J.A. Motyer, G.J. Wenham, *New Bible Commentary 21st Century Edition*. Illinois: Intervarsity Press, 1994.

Chrysostom, John, *Homilies on the Epistle of Paul to the Corinthians* 35.4, Available from http://www.ccel.org/ccel/schaff/npnf109.iii.i.html?highlight=ohn,chrysostom,homilies,on,the,epistle,of,paul,to,corinthians#highlight , accessed on 24 March 2010.

Clement. *First Epistle of Clement to Corinthians*, 1Clem 2:2 Available from http://www.earlychristianwritings.com/text/1clement-lightfoot.html , accessed on 24 March 2010.

"Did Augustine Speak in Tongues," *Grace Forums*, Available from http://www.graceforums.com/printthread.php?tid=2312 accessed on 19 April 2010.

Didache, 11:9-11. Available from http://www.earlychristianwritings.com/text/didache-lightfoot.html accessed 24 March 2010.

Dienstberger, Paul R., *The American Republic: A Nation of Christians*. (2000) Available from http://www.prdienstberger.com/nation/Chap2fga.htm#I.%20The%20Early%20Stirrings

Ekonomou, Andrew J. *Byzantine Rome and the Greek Popes: Eastern influences on Rome and the papacy from Gregory the Great to Zacharias, A.D. 590-752*. Maryland: Lexington Books, 2007.

Gee, Donald, *Concerning Spiritual Gifts*, Missouri, Gospel Publishing House, n.d.

Goll, Dr. James, The Fourth Great Wave of the Holy Spirit https://www.charismanews.com/opinion/56670-the-fourth-great-wave-of-the-holy-spirit-has-begun

Gospel of the Egyptians, The – *The Nag Hammadi Library. The Gnostic Society Library*. Available from http://www.gnosis.org/naghamm/goseqypt.html

Gregory the Great, GMI 455; Migne, PL 76:1169

Harkness, Gloria, *Mysticism, Its Meaning and Message,* Tennessee: Abingdon, 1973.

Harris, Ralph W., *Spoken by the Spirit: Documented Accounts of "Other Tongues" From Arabic to Zulu.* Missouri: Radiant Books, 1973.

Hollenweger, Walter J. "Pentecostalism's Global Language, It's not Tongues but a different way of being a Christian," *Christian History and Biography*, 1 April 1998, Issue 58. p. 42

Irenaeus, Against Heresies", Book V.

Irving, Edward, Facts Connected with Recent Manifestations of Spiritual Gifts, Frascer's Magazine for Town and Country, Vol 4), p. 760.

Johnson, Luke Timothy, *Religious Experience in the earliest Christianity: A Missing Dimension in New Testament Studies.* Minnesota: Augsburg Fortress, 1998.

Justin Martyr, Dialogue with Trypho, Chap LXXXII.

Kelsey, Morton T., *Tongue Speaking: An Experiment in Spiritual Experience.* New York: Doubleday & Company, 1964.

Lacy, John, *A Cry from the Desert,* London, 1708.

Lawrence, B.F. "A History of the Present Latter Rain Outpouring of the Holy Spirit Known as the Apostolic or Pentecostal Movement," The Weekly Evangel, 22 January 1916. http://enrichmentjournal.ag.org/200602/200602_078_AzusaDoctrine_84_RI.cfm

McBrien, Richard P. McBrien, Harold W. Attridge, *The Harper Collins Encyclopedia of Catholicism.* California: HarperSanFrancisco, 1995.

McClymond, Michael (Ed.), *Encyclopedia of Religious Revivals in America, Volume Two: Primary Documents.* Connecticut: Greenwood Press, 2007.

Milavec, Aaron Milavec, The Didache: Faith, Hope & Life of Earliest Christian Communities 50-70 C.E. New Jersey: The Newman Press, 2003.

Miller, Frederic P., Agnes F. Vandome and John McBrewster, *Continuationism: Christian theology, Christian, Spiritual gift, Glossolalia, Prophecy, Cessationism, Christian denomination, Catholic Church, Orthodox Church, Pope Paul VI, Pentecostalism, Charismatic Movement*, Pennsylvania: Alpha Publishing, 2009.

Mills, Watson E., *Speaking in Tongues: Let's Talk About It*, Texas: Word Books, 1973.

Murphy-O'Connor, Jerome, Good News Studies 6, St. Paul's Corinth Texts and Archaeology. Delaware: Michael Glazier, Inc., 1983.

Nikephoros, life of Andrew the Fool 2:87

Oden, Thomas C. Oden, *Ancient Commentary on Scripture. New Testament II, Mark,* Illinois: Intervarsity Press, 1998.

Origen, *Commentary on I Corinthians* 4.61-62.

Ozman, Agnes "When The Latter Rain First Fell: The First One to Speak in Tongues". In The Latter Rain Evangel, January 1909, p.2. Available online at http://pentecostalarchives.org/digitalPublications/ USA/Independent/Latter%20Rain%20Evangel/Un registered/1909/FPHC/1909_01.pdf

Plato, *Phaedrus*, available from http://classics.mit.edu/Plato/phaedrus.html

Rice, John R, *Commentary on I and II Corinthians, The Church of God at Corinth.* Tennessee: Sword of the Lord Publishers, 1973.

Saint Bede, *Ancient Christian Commentary on Scripture: New Testament XI, James, 1-2 Peter, 1-3 John, Jude.* Ed. Gerald Bray and Thomas C. Oden. Illinois: InterVarsity Press, 2000.

Saint Gregory the Great, Available from http://www.doctorsofthecatholicchurch.com/ GG.html

Saint Hildegard, *Scivias / Hildegard of Bingen,* New York: Paulist Press, 1990.

Sanford, William LA Sor, David Allan Hubbard, Frederic William Bush, and Leslie C. Allen William Sanford, Old Testament Survey: The

Message, Form, and Background of the Old Testament, Michigan: Wm Eerdmans Publishing, 1996.

Schaff, Philip, *Fathers of the Third and Fourth Centuries: Lactanius, Venantius, Asterius, Victorinus, Dionysius, Apostolic Teaching and Constitutions, Homily* Volume 7, available from http://www.ccel.org/ccel/schaff/anf07.v.ii.html

Schaff, Paul, *Creeds of Christendom with a History and Critical Notes, Volume I, The History of Creeds, The Catholic Apostolic Church (called Irvingites)* §113. Available from http://www.ccel.org/ccel/schaff/creeds1.html

Severian of Gabala. "Pauline Commentary from the Greek Church," *Ancient Commentary on Scripture, 1 & 2 Corinthians,* Eds Gerald Bray and Thomas C. Oden, Illinois: Dearborn Publishers, 1999.

Speaking in Tongues, Available from www.speaking-in-tongues.net

Synan, Vinson, *The Century of the Holy Spirit: 100 Years of Pentecostal and Charismatic Renewal 1901-2001*, Nashville, Thomas Nelson 2001

Tertullian, *Tertullianus Against Marcion: Ante Nicene Christian Library Translations of the Writings of the Fathers Down to AD 325,* Part Seven, Book V,

Chapter VIII, ed. Alexander Roberts, Montana: Kessinger Publishing, 2004.

Thomas, Charles et ano, *Vita Sancti Paterni:* The Life of Saint Pardarn. Trivium Publications, 2003

Thompson, Steve, *A Twentieth Century Apostle: A.G. Garr* from Morning Star Publications; 2004

Van Elderen, Bastian, "Glossolalia in the New Testament" *Bulletin of the Evangelical Theological Society* 7, no. 2 (1964) p.55-6 available from http://www.biblicalstudies.org.uk/pdf/bets/vol07/7-2_elderen.pdf,

Wesley, John, *The Works of the Rev. John Wesley in Ten Volumes*, Vol. IX. New York,

J. & J. Harper, 1827.

Williams, George, *The Radical Reformation,* Pennsylvania: Westminster Press, 1962.

ABOUT THE AUTHOR

Katherine Duke (K.D.) Johnson is a native New Yorker. She is an ordained minister at Kings Church in Charlotte, N.C. She is the author of two other books: ***On the Brink of Ministry*** and ***God's Method: Principles to Propel You into Your Life Call***. She was served as Professor of New Testament Studies and Church History at ORU satellite Charlotte location. She holds a BA from Nyack College and a MAR Christian from Gordon Conwell Theological Seminary. K.D. hosts a podcast ***#BeALady*** and as well as a YouTube Channel, ***Reading the Christian Classics with Min. Kate***.

K.D. currently resides in Charlotte, North Carolina with her husband Kirk.

---

https://www.facebook.com/kdjohnsoninc/

https://minkatemarie.podbean.com/

min.katemarie@gmail.com

Printed in Great Britain
by Amazon